A SIMPLIFIED GUIDE TO PROBATE JURISDICTIONS:

WHERE TO LOOK FOR WILLS

THIRD EDITION

Compiled by J.S.W. Gibson

Federation of
Family History Societies
1986

First published 1980 by the

Federation of Family History Societies,
31 Seven Star Road, Solihull, West Midlands B91 2BZ

Second edition, 1982, reprinted 1983

ISBN 0 907099 45 9

Printed by Parchment (Oxford) Limited

Acknowledgements

The information in this Guide is largely based on that in my earlier book, "Wills and Where to Find Them" (1974). At that time I visited nearly all the probate record holding offices and received a great deal of help from archivists throughout the country. For this simplified revision, I circulated all the record offices and once again received a generous response. I would like to acknowledge my gratitude to all those archivists who so willingly help their enquirers, and hope that this Guide will prove of use to them.

In these second and third editions I have again received much help from archivists, who have updated information and corrected minor errors. In particular the movement is recorded of Berkshire, Buckinghamshire and Oxfordshire probate records from the Bodleian to the appropriate county record offices, and of the records of the Dean and Chapter of Saint Paul's Cathedral to Guildhall Library, London. I am also grateful to Mr Patrick Smythe Wood for information on Irish probate records and their indexes.

The county maps showing probate jurisdictions are based on those in "Wills and Where to Find Them", which themselves were loosely based on the excellent series of county parish maps published by the Institute of Heraldic and Genealogical Studies, Northgate, Canterbury. These have benefitted countless genealogists, and serious researchers should acquire them for the counties in which they are interested.

At the request of my American distributor this edition does include a copyright notice, but, in recognition of the source of the information, record offices and family history societies are still welcome to reprint parts, with acknowledgment but no other requirement.

Contents

Introduction

As stated in its title, this is a **simplified** guide to probate jurisdictions and their records. It is designed for the newcomer to local and family history. Its purpose is to suggest where to **start** looking for wills and their associated records.

For this reason, information on location of probate records before the mid-16th century is largely omitted. Wills before this date are in any case relatively rare; and anyone who has successfully researched back to this time, or has decided to work on Tudor and earlier families, does not come into the category of 'beginner'. When users have exhausted the sources and indexes described in this guide, they too are no longer beginners. For further possible sources and for information on pre-Reformation jurisdictions, they should consult my earlier book, "Wills and Where to Find Them" (1974) or the even more detailed and authoritative "Wills and their Whereabouts" by Anthony J. Camp (1974). Although both are now out of print, copies of one or both are to be found in most reference libraries and record offices. The only major movements of probate records since 1974 have been of Hereford diocesan records from the National Library of Wales to Hereford, of Berkshire archdeaconry and of Oxford consistory and archdeaconry records from the Bodleian to the Berkshire and Oxfordshire Record Offices respectively, and of Middlesex records to the main Greater London Record Office. The developments of the past eleven years are indicated in this Guide.

As this is a guide to records of the nineteenth and earlier centuries, it has been logical to arrange it according to the counties as they existed before local government reorganisation in 1974. For the same reason local record offices are still maintained for counties, such as Huntingdon, which have been absorbed into larger administrative areas.

Wills since 1858

The crucial date for testamentary research in England and Wales is 1858, when the present centralised system was introduced. From this date, copies of all wills and letters of administration (admons., for people not leaving wills) are to be found at the Principal Registry of the Family Division, Somerset House, Strand, in central London. However, printed indexes to these are often held locally. Locations are given under each county heading and on pages 1 and 2. Registered copies of wills proved at district registries are now often held by local record offices, and such holdings are also shown under individual counties. In some cases original wills have been retained by the district registries (and are so indicated), but many collections have been deposited with the Public Record Office and are now at Hayes.

Before 1858

Before 1858, probate was handled by ecclesiastical courts, with jurisdiction in archdeaconries, dioceses of bishops (consistory courts) and provinces of the archbishops of Canterbury and York (prerogative courts, usually abbreviated to P.C.C. and P.C.Y.); there were also areas exempt from archidiaconal and episcopal jurisdiction, known as 'peculiars'.

Probate records of P.C.C. are now at the Public Record Office at Chancery Lane in central London; for fuller details of indexes, etc, see page 2. Wills and admons. of the important and wealthy, the nobility, gentry, landowners, prosperous merchants and tradesmen, and those that died overseas, are most likely to be found in this collection; but use of the court was by no means confined to such classes, so indexes to P.C.C. should still be searched however humble a testator may be thought to be.

P.C.C. had jurisdiction throughout England and Wales, though wills of testators from counties in the northern province of York (Cheshire, Cumberland, Durham, Flint (southern detachment), Lancashire, Northumberland, Nottinghamshire, Westmorland and Yorkshire) are more likely to be found in P.C.Y., see page 46.

Apart from P.C.C. and P.C.Y., probate records for any particular county in England are likely to be found at the county record office (acting as diocesan record office). The main exceptions are:

Cambridgeshire: Cambridge University Library.
Derbyshire: Joint Record Office, Lichfield.
Durham: Dept. of Palaeography and Diplomatic, University of Durham
London and Middlesex: mainly at Guildhall Library and Greater London Record Office.
Monmouthshire: National Library of Wales.
Rutland: Northamptonshire Record Office.
Shropshire: split between Hereford, Lichfield and the National Library of Wales.
Staffordshire: Joint Record Office, Lichfield.
Surrey: Greater London Record Office.
Warwickshire: split between Lichfield and Worcester.
Westmorland: split between Cumbria R.O., Carlisle, and Lancashire R.O., Preston.
Yorkshire: mainly at the Borthwick Institute, York; some at Leeds Archives Dept.
Wales: National Library of Wales.

Although the jurisdiction of the ecclesiastical courts was by archdeaconries and dioceses, these usually coincided with county boundaries and so make identification of court much easier than may at first appear. There are of course numerous exceptions, some affecting large or populous areas, many the occasional parish. It is the purpose of this guide to lead its users to the correct indexes and record offices both for places which fall within the expected jurisdictions and for those that are the exceptions.

Probate Documents and Procedures

Although there was a great variety of courts in which wills were proved the types of document produced by the process are basically the same whichever court was responsible. The main record is obviously the will, supplemented by an inventory of the deceased's goods and by grants of probate and administration.

Wills survive in two forms: the originals which were filed away after being exhibited in the probate court and the registered copy, being a transcription of the will made at the time of probate and bound into a large volume.

When a will is exhibited in the probate court and found to be valid a grant of probate is made to the executors. The grant is similar to the administration bond, which is taken out by a person or persons who are to administer the goods of someone who has died intestate. Both documents survive, like wills, in two forms. Firstly a record of the grant of probate or administration is made in the probate act books, the details noted generally including the name, condition (i.e. occupation - blacksmith, innholder, gent., etc.) and place of residence of the deceased, with similar information about the executors/administrators, and a note of their relationship, if any, to the deceased. Secondly, there are the bonds, which are signed by the executors/administrators and, as well as including the above information, also give the sum of money the executors/administrators are bound to forfeit if they do not fulfill their task to the satisfaction of the court. This sum is normally about twice the value of the deceased's personal estate. The bonds are filed away with the original wills.

When a person dies leaving children to be cared for the executors/administrators have to enter into tuition or curation bonds, which record the same information as the administration bond but, since they are bonds to look after the deceased's children rather than to administer his estate, they record the names of the children concerned. Again, these bonds survive in two forms. There are the originals, filed away with the wills and administration bonds and there are registered copies, which can either be in the probate act books or in a volume specifically kept for that purpose.

Inventories are lists of the deceased's goods and chattels exhibited in the probate court. In theory an inventory should accompany each will or grant of administration, but in practice, as might be expected, this is not always the case. Their survival varies from diocese to diocese and even from probate court to probate court within a single diocese. For the Prerogative Court of Canterbury they only survive in any quantity between 1661 and c.1700, but many local courts have good collections for the later sixteenth and the seventeenth centuries. In general later inventories are less informative and they die out in the eighteenth century.

[These notes on probate procedures and documents are based, by kind permission of the Borthwick Institute of Historical Research, on the Institute's "Guide to Genealogical Sources", by C.C. Webb, 1981.]

Glossary

Account: The 'true and just account' which executors or administrators sometimes had to render.

Act: The endorsement on a will indicating probate had been granted, the record of a grant in an act book.

Act Book: A day-by-day account of the official grants of probate of wills, letters of administration (admon.), and other testamentary business.

Administration, Letters of (usually abbreviated to **Admon.**): A grant to the next-of-kin (or some other person or persons) who applied to administer the property of an intestate.

Administration (Letters of) with Will annexed: A grant, usually to the next-of-kin, when the will did not specify any executors or they were unable to act, or renounced, or had died. The will is then attached to the admon. bond. Sometimes filed under admons. instead of wills.

Administrator: A man vested with the right to administer an estate, normally, in the case of an intestate, the next-of-kin; but one might be appointed when the executor, or next-of-kin, was a minor. An administratrix was a women.

Admon.: See **Administration, Letters of.**

Archdeaconry: Normally the lowest of the ecclesiastical courts with testamentary jurisdiction. In larger dioceses there might be several, often co-terminous with counties (cf. Berkshire in the diocese of Salisbury), whilst just one might cover the whole of a smaller diocese (cf. Oxford). It was not unusual for the bishop's consistory court to appropriate this jurisdiction (cf. Lichfield), of for a commissary to be appointed for an archdeaconry (cf. Buckingham in the diocese of Lincoln).

'Bona Notabilia': A Latin term meaning considerable goods, technically worth £5 and more. When the deceased had 'bona notabilia' in more than one jurisdiction, a will should have been proved in a superior court.

Bond: A signed and witnessed obligation, the conditions of which might include the proving of a will, administration of an intestate's estate, rendering an account or inventory, or guardianship of a minor.

Calendar: In this guide, this generally implies an index, chronological within initial letter, normally contemporary with the records. A modern fully alphabetical index is to be preferred.

Caveat: A warning notice that a will is to be disputed.

Citation: A summons to appear before a court.

Commissariot: In Scotland the district within the jurisdiction of a commissary court. In 1823 the old districts were abolished, and most commissariots thereafter coincided with the old sheriffdoms (counties) and the sheriff court districts, with which they were merged in 1876. See also **Sheriffdom** and **Sheriff Court.**

Commissary: A person who held authority or a commission to exercise jurisdiction on behalf of an archbishop, bishop or other dignitary; the title continued to be used in Scotland in spite of the abolition of episcopal authority.

Commissary Court: A court acting with delegated powers from the bishop, normally as a consistory court but in one archdeaconry only - in contrast to an archdeaconry court which was subject to the archdeacon. In Scotland, one of the courts which took over the jurisdiction of the pre-reformation church courts.

Confirmation: In Scotland, the completion of the probate of a testament by the executors.

Consistory Court: The bishop's ecclesiastical court, with superior jurisdiction to an archdeaconry court. Theoretically wills of testators with 'bona notabilia' in two archdeaconries within the same diocese would be proved in the consistory court, and often the wills of clergy were reserved to it. In many dioceses it displaced the archdeaconry court entirely (cf. Lichfield), or had jurisdiction over certain parishes exempt from the archdeacon's jurisdiction (cf. Canterbury). In large dioceses powers were often delegated from the consistory court of the diocese to commissary courts acting in different archdeaconries (cf. Buckingham in the diocese of Lincoln). The consistory court would normally have jurisdiction during periodic visitations of the bishop to different archdeaconries, when the archdeaconry court would be **inhibited.**

Curation: Guardianship over orphaned minors, under 21 but over 14 (boys) or 12 (girls). See also **Tuition.**

Dean (and Chapter): Clergy who were members of a cathedral chapter, often with peculiar jurisdiction over parishes in the patronage of that cathedral.

Diocese: The district over which a bishop has authority.

Executor (often abbreviated to **Exor.**): A man appointed by the testator to see that the provisions of a will are carried out. An executrix is a woman.

Grant: Approval of the submission of the executor or administrator, denoting probate or letters of administration.

Guardianship: See **Curation** and **Tuition.**

Honour: See **Manor.**

Inhibition: The period during the visitation of a bishop to an archdeaconry, when the archdeacon's court would be closed and probate business conducted in the consistory court. In theory the visitation of an archbishop to a diocese would have the same effect on a consistory court, but in post-medieval times this was likely to be 'pro forma' only. Some peculiars were entirely exempt from visitation and inhibition, others were subject to visitation by a dean or a dean and chapter. Visitations would normally last several months at intervals of several years.

Intestate: A person who died without making a will.

Inventory: A list of personal and household goods left by the deceased, with their appraised value. Occupation was usually given, or can be inferred from tools of trade. They were common in the later 16th and 17th centuries, but became much less detailed and frequent in the 18th century; except in Scotland where they continued to a much later date.

Jurisdiction: The area over which a court claimed the right to grant probate or letters of administration. Peculiars within this area would be exempt from the jurisdiction of the court concerned.

Letters of Administration: See **Administration.**

Liberty: See **Manor.**

Manor: Occasional manorial courts had peculiar or exempt jurisdiction over a parish or part of a parish. An **Honour** (cf. Knaresborough, Yorks.) or **Liberty** (cf. Frampton, Dorset) might be a group of manors with such exempt jurisidction.

Nuncupative Will: A will made orally, normally by a testator on his deathbed, written down and sworn to by witnesses, but not signed by the deceased.

Peculiar (Testamentary): A parish or group of parishes, not necessarily adjacent or even in the same district or county, which were usually exempt from the testamentary jurisdiction of the archdeaconry and often the consistory court. Ecclesiastical peculiars were often subject to a dean or dean and chapter, though they might be administered by a locally appointed official; a bishop's peculiar might be administered by the consistory court; a number were royal or archbishop's peculiars, usually locally administered; and there were some lay, manorial or collegiate, peculiars. See also **Inhibition.**

Personalty: Personal property (goods, chattels, credits, etc.) as opposed to **real property.** In Scotland, until 1868, and in the Channel Islands only personalty (moveable property) could be bequeathed, and a document so excluding **realty** is technically known as a **testament.**

Prebend: So far as testamentary matters are concerned, this was a type of ecclesiastical peculiar, in the jurisdiction of a prebendary, who was appointed by the dean and chapter of a cathedral; accordingly it was usually subject to their visitation and inhibition.

Prerogative Court: See **Province.**

Probate: Evidence that a will has been accepted and that the executor has been granted permission to carry out its provisions.

Proved: A will has been proved when probate has been granted.

Province: The dioceses over which an archbishop has authority, ie, before 1858, in England and Wales, the provinces of Canterbury and York, and in Ireland, the province of Armagh. The **prerogative courts** of the archbishops had superior jurisdiction to all others, and Canterbury was superior to York.

Realty, Real Property, Real Estate: Property or interests in land, as opposed to **personalty.** In Scotland, until 1868, and in the Channel Islands, realty (heritable property) could not be bequeathed, and in England there were certain limitations on its bequest, so that it does not always appear in wills.

Registers and Registered Wills: Volumes of copy wills, made at the time of probate. It is these the searcher will normally see, though sometimes only original wills are available. At times only the registered copies survive. These are not to be confused with archbishops' and bishops' registers, which record their provincial and diocesan activities, but also include occasional wills, particularly in medieval times.

Renunciation: When an executor declines to apply for probate.

'Sede Vacante': See **Vacancy.**

See: Often used as a synonym for **diocese,** though technically the seat of the bishop or the diocesan centre.

Sentences: The final judgment on a disputed will, often entered in an act book.

Sheriff Court: In Scotland, since 1876 the court with testamentary jurisdiction over anyone dying within its district, usually a county or part of a county. There are several such districts in each modern sheriffdom. Its official, the sheriff clerk, has custody of current testamentary records and also often of the 1823-1876 records of the commissariot court of the former sheriffdom, which the modern sheriff court district has replaced.

Sheriffdom: In Scotland, an administrative area, generally in the mid-19th century coinciding with a county, which between 1823 and 1876 acted as a commissariot district. In more recent years their number has been reduced and each now incorporates several counties and sheriff court districts. See also **Commissariot.**

Surrogate: A deputy appointed by the ecclesiastical court to deal with testamentary and other matters.

Testament: Normally a synonym for a **will,** but technically a document which excludes **realty** (heritable property), as in Scotland and the Channel Islands.

Testator: A man who has made a will. A testatrix is a woman.

Tuition: Guardianship over orphaned minors, under 15 (boys) or 13 (girls). See also **Curation.**

Vacancy: A break in the official business of the court on the death or translation of the bishop or other chief official. The court might be closed and business carried on in another court, but often this was 'pro forma' only, ie the same actual officials carried on, powers from the alternative court being delegated to them.

Warrants (of testaments): In Scotland, normally the drafts from which the entries in the register were made up, but occasionally including original wills.

Will: A written statement by which a person regulates the disposition of property and rights after his or her death, normally signed and witnessed. See also **Testament.**

Abbreviations

Admon.	-	Letters of Administration
BRS	-	British Record Society
C19	-	19th century
Inv.	-	Inventory
MS	-	Manuscript
SofG or SG	-	Society of Genealogists
SRS	-	Scottish Record Society
TS	-	Typescript

England and Wales

Since 1858: A centralised system for probate came into operation in England and Wales on 12 January 1858, with a principal probate registry in London and a chain of district registries in important centres. A similar system came into operation in Ireland at the same date (see page 60) and to an extent in Scotland in 1876 (see page 58). Testamentary matters for the Channel Islands and the Isle of Man are still in the jurisdiction of local courts.

In England and Wales a consolidated Index of Grants of probate and letters of administration within the year has been printed annually. Before 1870, admons. were listed separately at the end of volumes.

These indexes may be consulted without charge at the Principal Registry of the Family Division, Somerset House, Strand, London WC2R 1LP, tel. 01-405 7641, ext. 3959 (formerly known as the Principal Probate Registry). Copies of these annual indexes were sent to district registries, but those over 50 years old have in most cases been transferred to local record offices or libraries. Their present locations are listed below. They can be a useful short cut to finding the death of an adult even if the will is not immediately available.

There are copies of all these wills and admons. since 1858 at Somerset House. These may be consulted on payment of a small fee, and photocopies are obtainable. Records over one hundred years old may be consulted without charge by holders of a search permit, obtainable on prior application to the Record Keeper at Somerset House.

When probate was taken out at a district registry, that registry retained the original will and made a registered copy (in a bound volume) before forwarding a further copy to the Principal Registry. These registered copies have mostly been deposited at local record offices. In some cases district registries still retain the original wills, but often they have been sent to the Public Record Office repository at Hayes (to consult these and other original wills at the P.R.O., a week's notice is necessary). Until 1926 individual district registries only had jurisdiction in their own districts, in general coinciding with the counties in which they lay. There were none in the home counties. Present location of registered copies and originals if still held locally is given under each county.

Sets of the printed Indexes of Grants are located (as of Summer 1985) as below, in some cases including a few years later than those indicated:

Avon: Bristol Record Office, 1858-1900.

Cambs.: County Record Office (Cambs. C.C.), Huntingdon, 1858-1934.

Ches.: Cheshire Record Office, 1858-1929.

Cornwall: Bodmin Sub-Registry, Market Street, Bodmin PL31 2VW (tel. 0208 2279); for eventual transfer to the Cornwall Record Office, Truro.

Cumbria: Cumbria Record Office, Carlisle, 1858-1928.

Devon: Exeter Sub-Registry, 94 Fore St., Exeter EX4 3HZ (tel. 0392 74515).

Glos.: Gloucestershire Record Office, 1858-1929.

Gtr. Manchester: Greater Manchester Record Office, 56 Marshall Street, New Cross, Ancoats, Manchester M4 5FU (061 247 3383).

Hants.: Hampshire Record Office, Winchester, 1858-1932.

Lancs.: Lancashire Record Office, Preston, 1858-1928.

Leics.: Leicestershire Record Office, 1858-1886 (not in main record office, prior notice required); Leicester Probate Registry, Government Buildings, Newarke St., Leicester LE1 5SE, 1887 on.

Lincs.: Lincoln Sub-Registry, Mill House, Brayford Side North, Lincoln. Possibility of a transfer to Lincolnshire Archives Office.

Merseyside: Liverpool Record Office, 4th Floor, Brown Picton and Hornby Libraries, William Brown Street, Liverpool, 1858-1928.

Norfolk: Norwich Sub-Registry, 65 Cathedral Close, Norwich NR1 4DN (tel. 0603 26648).
Northants. - see Cambs.
Northumbd. - see Tyne and Wear.
Notts.: Nottinghamshire Record Office, 1858-1928.
Oxon.: Bodleian Library, Oxford (Lower Reading Room, Radcliffe Camera, on open shelves - readers' ticket necessary).
East Sussex: East Sussex Record Office, Lewes.
Tyne and Wear: Newcastle Registry, Plummer House, Croft St., Newcastle upon Tyne NE1 6NP (tel. 0632 328543).
West Midlands: Birmingham Reference Library, 1858-1928.
North Yorks: York Sub-Registry, Duncombe Place, York YO1 2EA.
South Yorks: South Yorkshire County Record Office, Sheffield, 1858-1900 (from Ipswich); 1900-1928 (from Sheffield).
West Yorks: West Yorkshire County Record Office, Wakefield, 1858-1928 (Leeds).
Dyfed: National Library of Wales, Aberystwyth, 1858-1972.
Dyfed Archives, Carmarthen, 1858-1928.
Glamorgan: Glamorgan Record Office, Cardiff, 1858-1928 (from Llandaff).
Gwynedd: Gwynedd Archives Service, Caernarfon, 1858-1929 (from Bangor).

District registries were also issued with a 16-volume set index to wills and admons. in P.C.C., 1853-1858. Copies of this are now located at:

Cambs. County Record Office, Huntingdon;
Exeter Sub-Registry;
Hampshire Record Office;
Kent Archives Office, Maidstone;
Leicestershire Record Office (prior notice required);
Lincoln Sub-Registry (possibility of transfer to Lincolnshire Archives Office);
Birmingham Reference Library;
Liverpool Record Office;
Nottinghamshire Record Office;
Oxford, Bodleian Library;
East Sussex Record Office, Lewes;
Tyne and Wear, Newcastle Registry;
York Sub-Registry;
South Yorkshire Record Office;
Dyfed, National Library of Wales, Aberystwyth;
Gwynedd Archives Service, Caernarfon.

ENGLAND AND WALES

Before 1858: As explained in the Introduction, probate records of the wealthy and important, particularly those with goods and property in more than one diocese, are likely to be found in the Prerogative Court of the archbishop rather than in the local consistory, archdeaconry or peculiar courts held in diocesan record offices. It is emphasised that these were not confined to such classes, and indexes to the higher courts are always worth searching, whatever standing the testator may be thought to have had.

The most important was the **Prerogative Court of Canterbury** (P.C.C.). This had over-riding jurisdiction in England and Wales, though few testators from the northern province of York in fact occur: for those counties (Cheshire, Cumberland, Durham, Flint (southern detachment), Lancashire, Northumberland, Nottinghamshire, Westmorland and Yorkshire) see the Prerogative Court of York (P.C.Y.)(page 46).

Wills of those dying overseas were also proved in P.C.C.

Records of **P.C.C.** are now at the

Public Record Office, Chancery Lane, London WC2A 1LR (01-405 0741)

Leaflet, "Probate Records", available. A Readers' ticket should be obtained beforehand. There is a special 'Wills Room' reached by going through the 'Long Room' and up the iron stairs, then straight ahead. On the open shelves of this room are the many volumes of printed indexes (wills to 1700, admons to 1660); contemporary MS calendars to 1852; and official printed index, 1853-1858 (10 January).

The registered copy wills, which are those normally seen by the searcher, are in P.R.O. class PROB.11, and are produced to readers on microfilm.

The individual years of probate were originally allocated names (based on that of some significant testator). These are quoted in many of the older printed indexes, and are on the spines of the MS calendars as well as the year. Once a will is located, with its year and number, a further list (of which there are copies adjacent to the shelves) must be consulted to identify the P.R.O. reference for the appropriate roll of microfilm. The number given in the index or calendar is that allocated to each gathering of 16 pages in the bound volumes, not to the later rubber stamped foliation numbers, so when spinning through the microfilm, the relatively occasional quire numbers have to be looked for. Once the system is understood it is easy enough to follow, and the P.R.O. staff are very helpful both in explaining this and the use of the microfilm readers.

Wills proved in P.C.C. date from 1383 and admons from 1559. The printed indexes to these are detailed below. During the Interregnum (1653-1660) this court, in the form of a civil institution, had sole jurisdiction in England and Wales, and effectively for the preceding ten years from the outbreak of the Civil War.

Indexes to P.C.C. wills (printed unless shown otherwise):

1383-1558	BRS 10 and 11
1558-1583	BRS 18
1584-1604	BRS 25
1605-1619	BRS 43
1620	"Register Soame", abstracts, by J.H. Lea, 1904
1620-1624	"Probates and Sentences", by J. and G.F. Matthews, 1911 (this contains additional references to BRS 44)
1620-1629	BRS 44
1630-1639	"Sentences and Complete Index Nominum" (surnames only), J. & G.F. Matthews
1630-1655	"Year Books of Probate" by J. and G.F. Matthews, vols. 1-8, 1903-27.
1630-1652	TS indexes to testators (full names) by P.Boyd at SofG.
1651	MS abstracts of Register Grey by Mrs A. Rowan, 15 vols., at SofG.
1653-1656	BRS 54
Jan. 1657/8-June 1658	"Register Wootton" by W. Brigg, 7 vols.
1657-1660	BRS 61
1661-1670	"Wills, Sentences and Probate Acts", J.H. Morrison, 1935
1671-1675	BRS 67
1676-1685	BRS 71
1686-1693	BRS 77
1694-1700	BRS 80
1750	"Register Greenly", by G. Sherwood, a list of all persons named, arranged in 8 groups, topographically - not indexed.
1750-1800	"Index to Wills proved in P.C.C.", ed. A.J. Camp, Soc. of Genealogists, A - G only, 1976, 1978, 1984. Further volumes in preparation. The Society will, for a fee, undertake searches in the complete card index, but this is not open for public search.
1853-1858	(10 Jan.) Consolidated index, with admons, in 16 vols. For location of other copies see page 2, column 1.

For the period 1701-1749 and 1801-1852 it is necessary to consult the contemporary MS calendars at the P.R.O.

Printed **indexes to P.C.C. admons.:**

1559-1580	"Administrations in P.C.C.", by R.M. Glencross, 2 vols., 1912-1917. TS corrigenda at P.R.O. MS index of places, 1559-1571 at SofG.
1581-1595	BRS 76
1596-1608	BRS 81
1609-1619	BRS 83
1620-1630	"Letters of Administration", by J.H. Morrison, 1934/5
1631-1648	BRS (in press)
1649-1654	BRS 68
1655-1660	BRS 72, 74, 75

From 1661 on it is necessary to consult the contemporary MS calendars, except 1853-1858, see above.

Inventories in P.C.C. rarely survive except for the period 1661-early 18th century. The very few pre-1661 (700) are listed at the P.R.O. (PROB.2).

1661-early C18 (6,105) 'paper' inventories in PROB.5, printed index (List & Index Soc., vol. 149).

1661-early C18 (26,060) 'parchment' inventories in PROB.4, TS list and slip index available only to 12,899 (and in progress).

1718-1760 (and a few to 1782)(5,500) in PROB.3, printed index (List & Index Soc., vols. 85 and 86).

(an article by myself on P.C.C. inventories appears in "The Local Historian", vol.14, no.4, November 1980).

For further information see "The Records of the Prerogative Court of Canterbury ...", a provisional guide by Jane Cox, P.R.O., 1980, £1.50.

There were two courts of appeal from P.C.C.: the P.R.O. has the records of **The Court of Delegates**, to which there is a printed index, wills and admons., 1651-1857 (550) in "The Genealogist" vols. 11 and 12.

Records of the second court of appeal from P.C.C., the **Court of Arches**, are at Lambeth Palace Library, London SE1 7JU. There is a printed index to wills, admons and invs (in disputed cases), 1660-1857 (BRS 85).

Also at the P.R.O., Chancery Lane, are the **Death Duty Registers**, another useful finding aid for those trying to locate the court in which a will or admon was recorded. They cover the years 1796 to 1894, but are only open to public inspection if over 125 years old.

They consist of abstracts of most, but by no means all, wills and admons, which had to be deposited at the Legacy Duty Department of the Stamp Office. For some areas they do not start until after 1800.

The indexes for the whole period are particularly valuable. Prior to 1812 they are arranged in three groups: P.C.C. wills, P.C.C. admons, and 'Country Courts', wills and admons, arranged court by court.

From 1812 the grouping alters and becomes vastly more useful, as **all** wills are indexed in one consolidated series, whatever the court. P.C.C. admons remain in a separate series; and all admons from the 'Country Courts' are indexed in a third (consolidated) series. The indexes are now on open shelves. They are confusingly laid out and before attempting to use them the P.R.O. leaflet 34 "Death Duty Registers" is essential reading.

Wills in the Public Record Office

As well as possessing numerous small collections of original or copy wills, the Public Record Office also contains some very large ones, quite apart from the P.C.C. and Stamp Office records mentioned above. Most of these probably appear in P.C.C. or some other court. The publication "List of Wills, Admons, etc, in the Public Record Office" (Magna Charta Book Co., 1968) is based on an unrevised TS in the Round Room dated 1932, and as a survey is both out of date and incomplete. Dr Cox in her guide to P.C.C. gives further possible sources.

Society of Genealogists, 14 Charterhouse Buildings, Goswell Road, London EC1M 7BA (01-251 8799).

The Society in its unique library and MSS collections includes virtually all printed indexes to wills and admons, much TS and MS material (including indexes), and thousands of abstracts. Of particular importance is its collection of microfilms of calendars of wills and admons - these were microfilmed by the Church of Jesus Christ of Latter-Day Saints some years ago, so usually are of 19th century and earlier indexes and calendars, which may well have been superseded since. Nevertheless they are useful for those able to get to London more easily than to the local record offices concerned.

The Society's collection in general is described definitively by A.J. Camp in "Wills and their Whereabouts", 4th edition (1974), so all but the barest details, under relevant counties, are omitted in this work.

Bedfordshire

Since 1858: Probate records for England and Wales are at the Principal Registry of the Family Division, Somerset House, Strand, London WC2R 1LP. For copies of the printed indexes elsewhere, see page 1.

Registered copy wills for Bedfordshire 1858-1930 are deposited at the Northamptonshire Record Office and are indexed to 1908.

Before 1858: Bedfordshire formed the archdeaconry of Bedford in the diocese of Lincoln and province of Canterbury.

Apart from P.C.C. (see page 2 and below), virtually all probate records for the whole county are at the

Bedfordshire Record Office (0234 63222).

One card index covers the **Archdeaconry of Bedford** and the two Peculiars of Biggleswade and Leighton Buzzard.
Wills 1480-1857, admons 1670-1857
Biggleswade Peculiar from 1720 only.
Leighton Buzzard Peculiar from 1701 only.

Exception:
Everton, in Archdeaconry of Huntingdon, see page 21.

Note. Although in the Diocese of Lincoln, consistory powers were delegated to the local Bedford court.

Printed sources

"Genealogia Bedfordiensis, 1538-1700" by F.A. Blaydes has numerous abstracts of Beds. wills arranged by parish.
"Bedfordshire Wills proved in the P.C.C. 1383-1548" (Beds. Hist. Record Soc. 58).

Places in Bedfordshire outside the jurisdiction of the archdeaconry (see map):

1. Everton (archdeaconry of Huntingdon)
2. Peculiar of Biggleswade
3. Peculiar of Leighton Buzzard:
   Leighton Buzzard and its former hamlets of
   Billington
   Eggington
   Heath and Reach
   Stanbridge

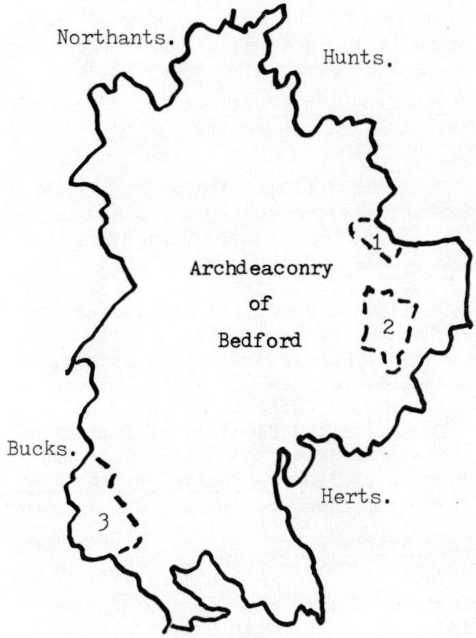

BEDFORDSHIRE

Berkshire

(north-western Vale of the White Horse now in Oxfordshire)

Since 1858: Probate records for England and Wales are at the Principal Registry of the Family Division, Somerset House, Strand, London WC2R 1LP. Indexes to these to 1928 are held locally at the Bodleian Library, Oxford (Radcliffe Camera, Lower Reading Room).

Before 1858: Berkshire formed the archdeaconry of Berkshire in the diocese of Salisbury and province of Canterbury. In 1836 the archdeaçonry was transferred to the diocese of Oxford.

The Society of Genealogists has, in the Snell collection, a MS list of Berkshire wills in **P.C.C.** 1631-1807 (vols. 16 and 21) with complete abstracts 1391-1737 (in 15 vols.) and a 25 vol. index of names and places.

Berkshire, continued

Apart from P.C.C. (see pages 2 and 5), most probate records for the county are now at the Berkshire Record Office; but there are also some at the Wiltshire Record Office; the Oxfordshire Record Office; and a few at Windsor Castle.

Records of the **Archdeaconry of Berkshire** (which covered all parishes except those listed right) are now at the

Berkshire Record Office, Shire Hall, Shinfield Park, Reading RG2 9XD (0734 875444 ext 3182).

There are printed indexes to these **Berkshire Archdeaconry** wills and admons 1508-1652 (BRS 8 and Oxford Hist Soc 23) and to all probate records 1653-1710 (BRS 87). Computerised index 1711-1857.

There were Peculiars centred around Faringdon, Wantage, West Ilsley, Blewbury, Hungerford and Wokingham, whose records are now split between three record offices.

Those for the **Peculiar of Faringdon** (Great Faringdon and Little Coxwell) are also now at the Berkshire Record Office. Those for **Langford** (partly Oxon) are at

Oxfordshire Record Office, County Hall, New Road, Oxford (0865 815203).

Records of both peculiars are jointly indexed (in MS) with Oxfordshire and Buckinghamshire peculiars, in one series, 1547-1853 (microfilm copy at Berkshire Record Office). Records for **Wantage**, 1582-1668, are also at the Oxon. R.O. and included in this index, but later records are at the Wilts. R.O.

Wiltshire Record Office, Trowbridge (022-14 3641 ext 3502)

holds probate records for the **Consistory Court of Salisbury**, 1526-1857. Some Berkshire testators are to be found in this court, which had superior jurisdiction to the archdeaconry court of Berkshire. There is a MS index compiled in the 19th cent., but this is being superseded by a very wide-ranging card index being compiled at the Record Office.

Records of two **peculiars** including Berkshire parishes are at the Wiltshire Record Office:

Wantage (Dean and Canons of Windsor in) (Hungerford, West Ilsley, Shalbourne and Wantage). MS and card index to all records from 1669 only to 1840. For records of Wantage and its hamlets (only) 1582-1668, see Oxfordshire Record Office.

Dean of Salisbury (Arborfield, Blewbury with Aston Upthorpe, Hurst, Ruscombe, Sandhurst, Sonning and Wokingham; also occasionally places in peculiars of Faringdon and Wantage). MS and card index to all records 1538-1857. See also a TS index to **Miscellaneous Wills** 1555-1730 of which many relate to this court.

There is a tiny collection of wills 1396-1736 for the **Court of the Dean of Windsor**, at

The Aerary, St. George's Chapel, Dean's Cloister, Windsor Castle, Berks. (07535 68286).

These relate only to a few inhabitants of the castle.

Berkshire parishes outside the jurisdiction of the archdeacon of Berkshire.

Peculiars: F - Faringdon; S - Dean of Salisbury; W - Dean and Canons of Windsor in Wantage

Arborfield S6; Aston Upthorpe S3; Blewbury S3; Little Coxwell F1; Great Faringdon F1; Hungerford W5; Hurst S6; West Ilsley W4; Ruscombe S6; Shalbourne (part Wilts.) W5; Sonning S6; Upton S3; Wantage W2; Wokingham S6.

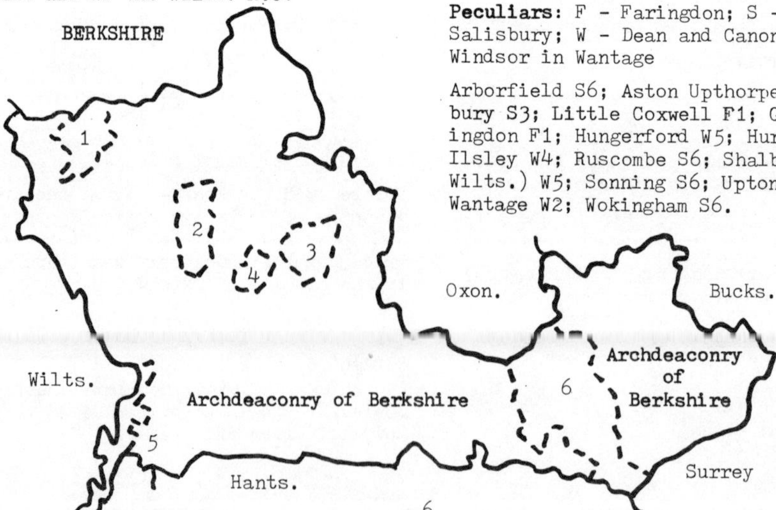

Buckinghamshire

(southern tip now in Berkshire)

Since 1858: Probate records for England and Wales are at the Principal Registry of the Family Division, Somerset House, Strand, London WC2R 1LP. Indexes to these (to 1928) are held locally at the Bodleian Library, Oxford; see also page 1.

Before 1858: Buckinghamshire formed the archdeaconry of Buckingham in the diocese of Lincoln and province of Canterbury.

Apart from P.C.C. (see page 2), most probate records for the county are at

Buckinghamshire Record Office, Aylesbury (0296 5000 ext 586)

and are described in a leaflet "Notes for the Guidance of Genealogists". The **Archdeaconry of Buckingham** covered virtually the whole county apart from peculiars. There is a card index to all probate records, wills 1483-1857, admons 1632-1857.

"The Courts of the Archdeaconry of Buckingham 1483-1523" (Bucks Record Society 19, 1975) includes many wills.

Records of most **Peculiars**, formerly at Oxford, are now also at the Bucks. R.O. These included Aylesbury and Buckingham, and other places listed right. All probate records are indexed jointly with Oxfordshire and Berkshire peculiars in a good 19th cent. index (MS at Oxon. R.O., microfilm at Bucks. R.O.), in theory from 1547 but in fact most commence much later (Aylesbury 1624, Buckingham few pre-1701).

Records of the **Peculiar of Bierton** (incl. also Buckland, Stoke Mandeville and Quarrendon), indexed as above, mostly are at the

Oxfordshire Record Office, County Hall, New Road, Oxford (0865 815203)

though register copy wills 1701-1708 and 1851-1857 are now at the Bucks. R.O.

The present or former Bucks parishes of Caversfield, Ipstone, Lillingstone Lovell and Stokenchurch were in the diocese and archdeaconry of **Oxford**, records at the Oxon. R.O., see page 33.

Hertfordshire Record Office (0995 555105) has records of Aston Abbots, Granborough, Little Horwood and Winslow, in the **Archdeaconry of St Albans** (see page 20). A list is held by the Bucks FHS for eventual publication. These places may also be found in the **Consistory Court of London** (page 26).

The only other probate records for Buckinghamshire are a small collection, Eton parishioners only, 1457-1666, kept at 'Penzance', Eton College, Berks.

Buckinghamshire parishes outside the jurisdiction of the archdeacon of Buckingham:

A : Archdeaconry of St Albans
B : Peculiar of Bierton (Bodleian)
O : Diocese and Archdeaconry of Oxford
P : Other Peculiars (Bucks. R.O.)

Aston Abbots A4; Aylesbury P6; Bierton B7; Buckingham P2; Buckland B9; Caversfield (det.) O; Eton 14; Granborough A3; Halton P10; Little Horwood A3; Ibstone or Ipstone O-13; Lillingstone Lovell O-1; Monks Risborough P12; Quarrendon B5; Stoke Mandeville B8; Stokenchurch O-13; Towersey P11; Winslow A3.

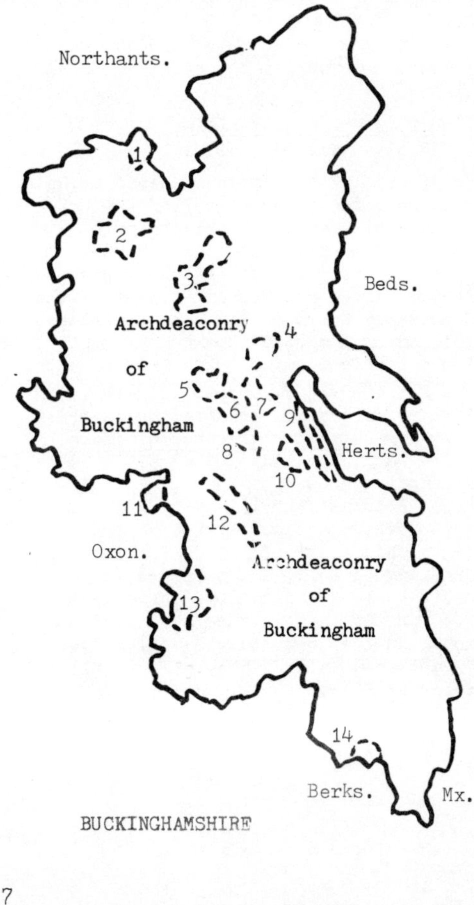

BUCKINGHAMSHIRE

Cambridgeshire and the Isle of Ely

See "Genealogical Sources in Cambridgeshire" by Michael Farrar, Cambs. R.O., 1979 (o.p., revision in progress).

Since 1858: Probate records for England and Wales are at the Principal Registry of the Family Division, Somerset House, Strand, London WC2R 1LP. Indexes to these (to 1934) are held locally at the County Record Office (Cambridgeshire C.C.), Huntingdon; for other copies, see page 1.

Registered copy wills proved at Peterborough, 1858-1941 (Cambridgeshire, Huntingdonshire and northern Northamptonshire to 1926) are deposited at the Northamptonshire Record Office, and are indexed.

Before 1858: Cambridgeshire was in the province of Canterbury and diocese of Ely.

Apart from P.C.C. (see page 2), most probate records for the county are held at the

<u>Cambridge University Library</u>
(0223 61441 ext 344/345)

Prior application for a readers' ticket must be made to The Keeper of the University Archives, The University Library, West Road, Cambridge CB3 9DR.

Of the two main collections of probate records, much the larger is that of the **Consistory Court of Ely** (and Cambridge). This covered most of the county, with the exceptions noted below and opposite.

Wills 1449-1857, admons 1562-1857, invs (TS index for publication by BRS; copy at <u>Cambridgeshire Record Office</u>, <u>Shire Hall, Cambridge (0223 317281)</u>). Printed: Admons 1562-1582 ("Ely Episcopal Records", pp.154-84).

The other main collection is that of the **Archdeaconry of Ely**, which included Cambridge itself, and parishes in the south-west of the county. Note that records for these places may also be found in the Consistory Court, above.

Published index: 1513-1857 (to all records)(BRS 88).

Continued on page 9

Archdeaconry of Ely ('7' on map unless otherwise stated):

Cambridge (all parishes) 6; Abington Pigotts; Bassingbourn; Bourn; Boxworth; Caldecote; Caxton; Cherry Hinton 6; Conington; Croxton; Croydon cum Clopton; Elsworth; Eltisley; Gt and Lit Eversden; Fen Drayton; Fulbourn 6; Gamlingay; Guilden Morden; Graveley; Haddenham 5; East Hatley; Hatley St George; Kingston; Knapwell; Litlington; Lolworth; Longstowe; Melbourn; Meldreth; Papworth St Agnes and Everard; Shingay; Steeple Morden; Swavesey; Tadlow; Toft; Wendy with Shingay; Whaddon; Wilburton 5.

Parishes outside the jurisdiction of the Consistory Court of Ely:

Archdeaconry of Sudbury, 4
Ashley cum Silverley; Burwell; Cheveley; Chippenham; Wood Ditton; Fordham; Kennett; Kirtling; Landwade; Newmarket All Saints; Snailwell; Soham; Wicken.

Archdeaconry of Norfolk, 2
Outwell, Upwell, Welney.

Peculiars of Isleham, 3, **and Thorney**, 1

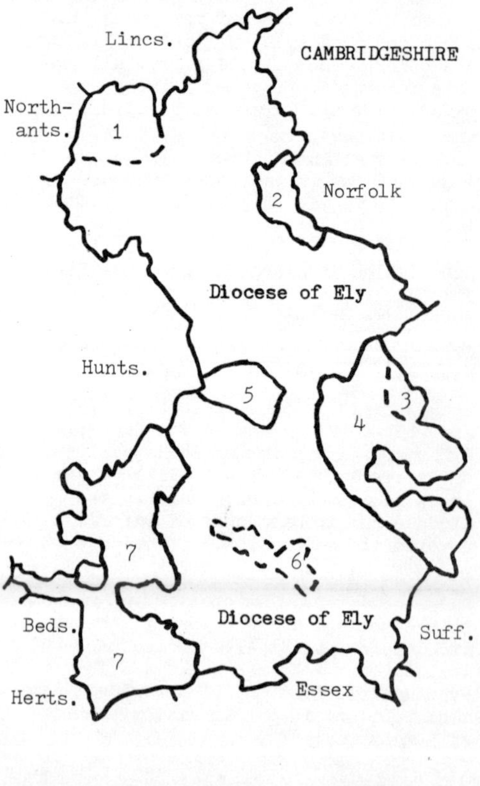

Cambridgeshire continued

Also at Cambridge University Library are the records of the **Court of the Chancellor (or Vice-Chancellor) of the University of Cambridge.** This was confined to members of the university and others connected with it, including some Cambridge townspeople.

Card index to all records 1501-1765 (note that this supersedes the published "Wills Proved in the Vice-Chancellor's Court at Cambridge", which is unreliable).

There are two other small collections at the Cambridge University Library:

Peculiar of Thorney
1774-1857 (calendar to all records)

Court of the Dean and Chapter of Ely
Confined to Ely Cathedral Close
1565-1800 (to be included in BRS Consistory Court index volumes).

Another small collection is at King's College, Cambridge, for the **Peculiar of King's College, Cambridge,** 1449-1794, confined to the precincts of King's College.

Probate records for parishes around Newmarket on the east of the county in the **Archdeaconry of Sudbury** are at the Suffolk Record Office, Bury St Edmunds. Modern indexes, 1439-1857 (pubd. to 1700, BRS 95,96), to all records, see page 39.

Also at this office are records of the **Peculiar of Isleham** (Cambs.) **and Freckenham** (Suffolk), for which there is a card index, 1556-1581, 1613-1636, 1647-1857 (admons, invs from 1662 only), pre-1701 entries also in BRS 95,96.

Records for these parishes may also be found in the consistory courts of Norwich (page 28), Rochester (page 22) and (after 1649) the archdeaconry court of Huntingdon (page 21).

Records of three parishes in the north-east of the county, Outwell, Upwell and Welney, in the **Archdeaconry of Norfolk,** are at Norfolk Record Office. There are published indexes to wills 1453-1602; see page 28 for these and other indexes.

Cheshire, continued

See also "Stockport Probate Records, 1578-1619", ed. C.B. Phillips and J.H. Smith, RS of Lancs & Ches vol.124 (1985).

Cheshire

(northern border now in Greater Manchester; Wirral in Merseyside)

Since 1858: Probate records for England and Wales are at the Principal Registry of the Family Division, Somerset House, Strand, London WC2R 1LP. Indexes to these are held locally by Cheshire R.O. (to 1929) and Greater Manchester R.O. For other copies, see page 1.

Registered copy wills proved at Chester, 1858-1940 (Cheshire only to 1926), are deposited at Cheshire R.O. and are indexed. Original wills 1858-1969 are at Chester Probate Sub-Registry, 17 Cuppin St, Chester CH1 2DA (0244 20997).

Before 1858: Cheshire was in the diocese of Chester and province of York - for P.C.Y., see p.46; for P.C.C., see p.2.

Apart from P.C.Y. and P.C.C. all probate records for the county are held at

Cheshire Record Office, Duke Street, Chester CH1 1RL (0244 602574)

The office issues leaflets on sources including probate records. The **Consistory Court of Chester** covered the entire county from the creation of the diocese in 1541. There are no peculiars in the county.

Indexes have been published by the Lancs. & Ches. Record Soc. to wills and admons, 1545-1837, with the prospect of further volumes to come.

Meanwhile there is a TS index to the remaining years, 1838-1857.

In this diocese only, estates worth less than £40 were kept in a separate 'infra' series, and in the published index volumes are in a separate volume before 1665, and in appendices from 1660 to 1800. Since 1800 they have been indexed jointly with the main series. To 1820 Cheshire and Lancashire wills and admons are intermingled in the indexes, but from 1821 they are in separate sections in each volume.

Lancs. & Ches. Record Soc. vols.:
1545-1650 (main series), 2 and 4
1590-1665 (infra series), 52
1660-1800, 15,18,20,22,25,37,38,44,45
1801-1820, 62,63,78
1821-1837 (Cheshire separate), 107,113, 118,120.

Vols. 33,43,52 list miscellaneous wills 1487-1800; and additional wills and admons for 1670 and 1693 are in vol. 63.

For a map of the county, see page 46.

Cornwall

Since 1858: Probate records for England and Wales are at the Principal Registry of the Family Division, Somerset House, Strand, London WC2R 1LP. Indexes to these are held locally by the Probate Sub-Registry, Market St., Bodmin (tel. 0208 2279). For other copies, see p.1.

Registered copy wills proved at Bodmin, 1858-1941 (only Cornwall to 1926) are deposited at the Cornwall Record Office, and are indexed by parish to 1929. Original wills, 1858-1969, are still at Bodmin Probate Sub-Registry.

Before 1858: Cornwall formed the archdeaconry of Cornwall in the diocese of Exeter and province of Canterbury.

Apart from P.C.C. (see page 2), most probate records for the county are at

Cornwall Record Office, Truro
(0872 73698)(appointment essential)
See "Guide to Cornish Probate Records", Cornwall R.O., 1984, £3.50 + 75p p&p.

These mainly comprise the **Consistory Court of the Archdeaconry of Cornwall**, printed index to wills and admons 1600-1799 (and a very few pre-1600)(BRS 56, 59); these also include the tiny **Royal Peculiar of St Buryan** 1600-1799 (in a separate section). This published index has been superseded at the C.R.O. by a card index with fuller and additional information, itself for eventual complete publication: 1600-1649 (four parts, A-D, E-K, L-R, S-Z, pub. 1985-6), £2.00 each part + 50p p&p. There is a separate MS index to St Buryan records.

For 1800-1857 there is a consolidated TS index, which also includes Estate Duty Office wills and admons for courts whose records have been destroyed (see below), 1812-1857. This index has been published on microfiche by BRS.

Records of the **Episcopal Consistory Court of Exeter** and **Episcopal Principal Registry of Exeter** were destroyed by enemy action in 1942. These courts had some jurisdiction throughout the county (particularly over clergy) and included all records for 22 Cornish parishes in peculiars (listed opposite). The lost records are indexed in BRS 35 (Principal Registry) 1559-1799, and BRS 46 (Consistory) 1532-1800.

Records of the **Peculiars of the Dean and Chapter of Exeter**, which included five Cornish parishes (see opposite), were also destroyed. See Glencross's calendar at Soc. of Gen., opposite.

Post-1811 Estate Duty Office copies of wills and admons from these courts are now at the Cornwall Record Office. Abstracts of wills and admons, 1796-1811, for these and other courts should still be found in Estate Duty Registers at the Public Record Office, page 4. The Devon and Cornwall Record Society has a microfilm of the index to these.

The Society of Genealogists has a TS calendar to Cornish wills and admons (mainly pre-1814, ?incomplete) in P.C.C. and Exeter courts, compiled before 1942 by J.R.M. Glencross.

Parishes in peculiars:
B = Bishop of Exeter; **D** = Dean and Chapter of Exeter; **S** = St Buryan

St Agnes D5; St Anthony in Roseland B7; Boconnock with Bradoc D3; St Breoke B2; Budock B6; (St) Buryan S8; Egloshayle B2; St Erney B4; St Ervan B2; St Eval B2; Falmouth B6; (St) Germans B4; (St) Gerrans B7; St Gluvias B6; St Issey B2; Landrake B1; Lawhitton B1; St Levan S8; Lezant B1; Mabe B6; St Merryn B2; Mylor B6; Padstow B2; Perranzabulo D5; Little Petherick (or St Petroc Minor) B2; South Petherwyn B1; Sennen S8; Trewen B1; St Winnow D3

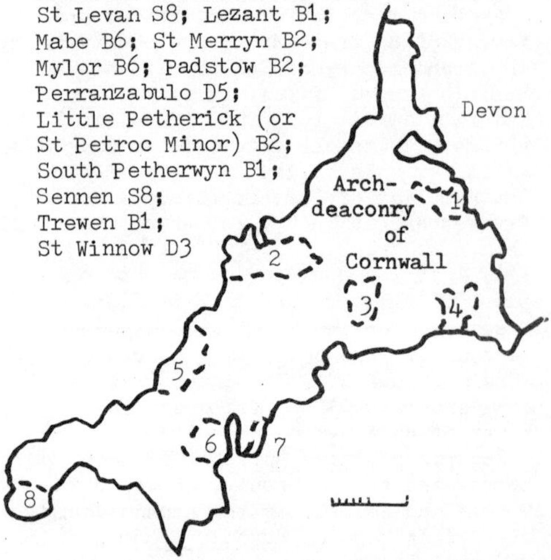

Cumberland and Westmorland

(now both in Cumbria)

Since 1858: Probate records for England and Wales are at the Principal Registry of the Family Division, Somerset House, Strand, London WC2R 1LP. Indexes to these (to 1928) are held locally at the Cumbria Record Office, Carlisle.

Cumberland and **Westmorland** continued

Registered copy wills proved at Carlisle (only Cumberland and Westmorland to 1926) are deposited at the Cumbria Record Office, Carlisle, and are indexed. Original wills, 1858-1969, are at the Carlisle Probate Sub-Registry, 2 Victoria Place, Carlisle CA1 1ER (tel. 0228 21751).

Before 1858: Cumberland and Westmorland were in the dioceses of Carlisle and Chester and in the province of York. For records of P.C.Y., see page 46. and also records of P.C.C., page 2.

Apart from P.C.Y. and P.C.C., the probate records for these two counties are split between Carlisle and Preston.

Cumbria Record Office, Carlisle (0228 23456)
holds records of the **Consistory Court of Carlisle**, which had jurisdiction over the major part of Cumberland and the northern half of Westmorland. See "Guide to Family History Records and Sources" (in preparation).

There is a card index to all probate records 1621-44, 1661-1796. Pending completion, MS indexes most be consulted for periods outside these dates.

Card indexes to manorial courts:
Ravenstonedale, 1691-1857
Temple Sowerby, 1580-1816
Docker, 1696-1770 (a few only)

Lancashire Record Office, Preston
holds records of the **Consistory Court of the Commissary of the Archdeaconry of Richmond (Western Deaneries)**, which had jurisdiction over the remainder of the two counties, the south-west of Cumberland (deanery of Copeland) and the southern part of Westmorland (deaneries of Kendal and Lonsdale, both partly in Lancashire).

There is a 19th cent. MS index to wills and admons, 1457-1720, and a calendar to the remainder, 1720-1857. Lists of Cumberland (deanery of Copeland) wills 1530-1726 are also at the Cumbria Record Office branches at Carlisle and Kendal. The indexes to the western deaneries printed by the Lancs. and Cheshire Record Society do not include non-Lancashire wills.

Exception:
Alston and Garrigill, and (until 1703) Upper or Over Denton, all in Cumberland, were in the jurisdiction of the **Consistory Court of Durham**, see page 15.

Parishes outside the jurisdiction of the consistory court of Carlisle:

Archdeaconry of Richmond, diocese of Chester:

Cumberland (Deanery of Copeland), 4
Arlecdon, Beckermet St Bridget and St John, Bootle, Brigham, Buttermere, Cleator, Clifton, Cockermouth, Corney, Dean, Distington, Drigg, Egremont, Embleton, Ennerdale, Eskdale, Gosforth, Harrington, Hensingham, Irton, Lamplugh, Lorton, Loweswater, Millom, Moresby, Mosser, Muncaster, Ponsonby, St Bees, Setmurthy, Thwaites, Ulpha, Waberthwaite, Wasdalehead, Nether Wasdale, Whicham, Whitbeck, Whitehaven, Workington, Wythop.

Westmorland (Deaneries of Kendal and Lonsdale), 5
Ambleside, Barbon, Beetham, Burnside, Burton in Kendal, Casterton, Crook, Crosthwaite, Firbank, Grasmere, Greyrigg, Holme, New and Old Hutton, Hutton Roof, Hugill (Ings), Kendal, Kentmere, Killington, Kirkby Lonsdale, Langdale, Mansergh, Middleton, Preston Patrick, Rydal, Selside, Long Sleddale, Over Staveley, Troutbeck, Underbarrow, Windermere, Winster, Witherslack.

Diocese of Durham: Alston with Garrigill, Cumb., 2; Upper Denton, Cumb., 1.

Peculiar of Ravenstonedale, 6.
Peculiar of Temple Sowerby, 3.

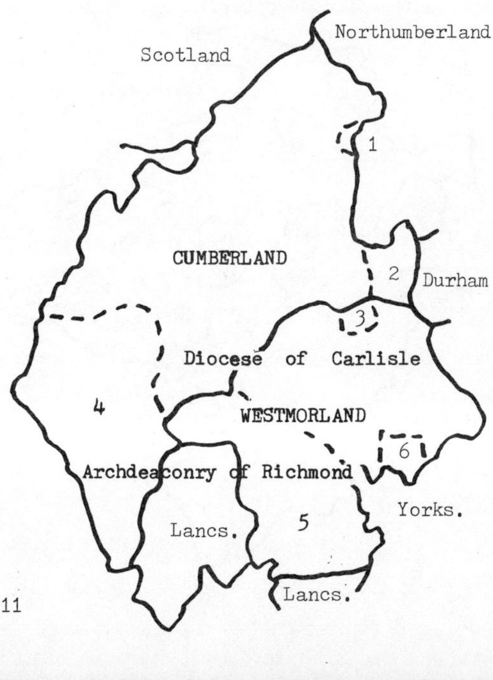

Derbyshire

See with **Staffordshire**, pages 36-38.

Devon

Since 1858: Probate records for England and Wales are at the Principal Registry of the Family Division, Somerset House, Strand, London WC2R 1LP. Indexes to these are held locally at the Probate Sub-Registry, 94 Fore Street, Exeter EX4 3HZ (tel. 0392 74515). For other copies, see page 1.

Before 1858: Devon was in the province of Canterbury and diocese of Exeter.

Apart from P.C.C. (see page 2), all probate records for the county and the diocese of Exeter (except Cornwall) were destroyed by enemy action in 1942.

Prior to this calamity, indexes to wills and admons in three important courts had been published. These were:
Episcopal Consistory Court of Exeter, 1532-1800 (BRS 46), jurisdiction throughout the county.
Episcopal Principal Registry of Exeter, 1599-1799 (BRS 35), jurisdiction throughout the county and sole jurisdiction in 14 Devon parishes which were peculiars of the bishop.
Consistory Court of the Archdeaconry of Exeter, 1547-1799 (BRS 35), jurisdiction in that archdeaconry.

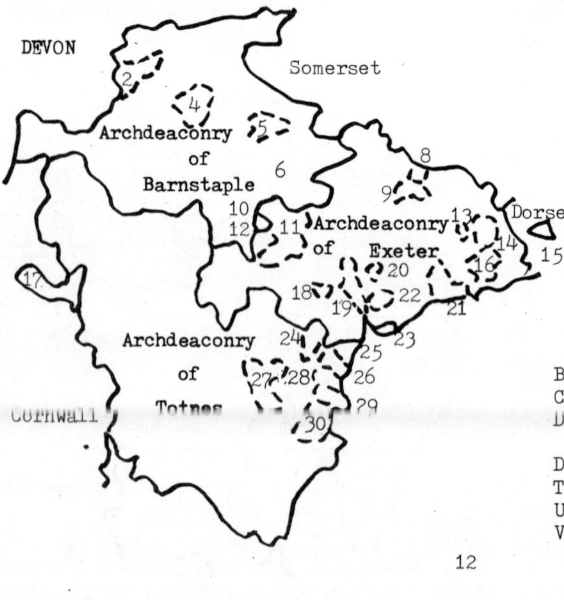

Copies of a TS index to the lost wills and admons of the **Consistory Court of the Archdeaconry of Barnstaple,** 1563-1857, are at the Westcountry Studies Library (Exeter Central Library), Exeter University, the North Devon Atheneum at Barnstaple, and New York Public Library.

No index survives to the lost records of the **Archdeaconry of Totnes.**

Devon Record Office, Exeter
(0392 273509)
(Family History leaflet available) has a large and partially indexed collection of copies of wills from numerous sources, particularly those made by Miss Moger. It also has Estate Duty Office copy wills from all Devon courts, 1812-1857. The Westcountry Studies Library has collections by Miss Moger and Oswyn Murray.

Wills and admons 1796-1811 should be found in the Estate Duty Registers at the Public Record Office, page 4. The Devon and Cornwall Record Society has a microfilm of the index to these Estate Duty Office abstracts.

There are also copies of wills at the West Devon Record Office, Plymouth.

Records for a few places not deposited at the destroyed Exeter Probate Registry include:

Cornwall Record Office, Truro
North Petherwin, St Giles in the Heath and Werrington, in the **Consistory Court of the Archdeaconry of Cornwall,** p.10.

Dorset Record Office
Stockwood and Dalwood (detached Dorset parishes) in **Consistory Court of Bristol (Dorset Division)** and **Archdeaconry of Dorset**, see page 13.

Wiltshire Record Office
Uffculme, in the **Prebend of Uffculme**, 1552-1857 (MS index); see also page 43.

Key to jurisdictions of places listed on page 13.

AC : Archdeaconry of Cornwall;
AD : Archdeaconry of Dorset;
AE : Archdeaconry of Exeter (outlying parishes);
BE : Bishop of Exeter's Peculiars;
C : Manor of Cockington
DC : Dean and Chapter of Exeter's Peculiars;
DE : Dean of Exeter's Peculiar;
T : Manor of Templeton;
U : Prebend of Uffculme
VC : Peculiar of Vicars Choral

Devon continued

Parishes in Devon outside the jurisdiction of the archdeaconries of Barnstaple, Exeter and Totnes. For key, see page 12.

Ashburton DC27; Bickington DC27; Bishops Nympton BE5; Bishops Tawton BE4; Bishops Teignton BE26; Branscombe DC21; Braunton DE2; Buckland-in-the-Moor DC27; Chudleigh BE24; Clyst Honiton DC20; Cockington C30; Coffinswell DC29; Colebrook DC12; Colyton DC16; Combeinteignhead AE28; Crediton BE11; Culmstock DC8; Dalwood AD&AE14; Dawlish DC25; Down St Mary AE10; Exeter Cathedral Close DE; Exmouth DC23; Heavitree DC19; Ide DC18; Kennerleigh BE11; Kingskerswell DC29; Landkey BE4; Littleham (nr Exmouth) DC23; Marldon BE29; Monkton DC13; Morchard Bishop BE11; Northcott AC17; E & W Ogwell AE28; Paignton BE30; N Petherwin AC17; St Giles in the Heath AC17; St Marychurch DC29; Salcombe Regis DC21; Sandford BE11; Shaldon AE28; Shute DC16; Sidbury DC21; Staverton DC27; Stockland AD&AE14; Stoke Canon DC19; Stoke Gabriel BE30; Stokeinteignhead AE28; Swimbridge BE4; East Teignmouth DC25; West Teignmouth BE26; Templeton T6; Thorncombe AE&AD15; Topsham DC19; Uffculme U9; Werrington AC17; Woodbury VC22.

Dorset

Since 1858: Probate records for England and Wales are at the Principal Registry of the Family Division, Somerset House, Strand, London WC2R 1LP. Indexes to these are held locally at the Bristol Record Office (to 1900); Exeter (probably Devon County Library; pre-1930); and the Hampshire Record Office, Winchester (to 1928); for other copies, see page 1.

Registered copy wills proved at Blandford, 1858-1941, are deposited at the Dorset Record Office and are indexed.

Before 1858: Dorset formed the archdeaconry of Dorset in the diocese of Bristol and province of Canterbury.

Indexes to **P.C.C.** wills for Dorset, 1383-1700 (printed) and 1701-1820 (MS); and admons 1559-1725 (printed, Somerset & Dorset Notes & Queries, vols. 2-6) and 1726-1821 (MS), all included in card index at Dorset Record Office; copy of these indexes at SofG. See page 2.

Apart from P.C.C., most probate records for Dorset are held at the

Dorset Record Office, Dorchester (0305 63131 ext 4411).

There is a consolidated card index to **all** these, including **all** local courts as well as P.C.C. before 1858, and the later Dorset Probate Registry records. This supersedes the various printed indexes (usually to all records).

The main courts for the county were the **Archdeaconry Court of Dorset** (ptd index 1660-1792 BRS 22, pp.25-179) and the much smaller **Consistory Court of Bristol (Dorset Division)**, which only had occasional jurisdiction (index 1681-1792 BRS 22, pp.1-24). A few records of these two courts will also be found in BRS 53 (pp.131-70). All card indexed to 1857.

There are also published lists or indexes, in BRS 22, to various Peculiars whose records are at the Dorset Record Office:

Great Canford and Poole, 1639-1799
Corfe Castle, 1577-1799
Milton Abbas, 1675-1811
Sturminster Marshall, 1641-1799
Wimborne Minster, 1590-1823 (also invs 1587-1719, in BRS 53, pp.129, described mistakenly as belonging to Great Canford and Poole).

There were numerous other peculiar courts in Dorset whose records are now at the Wiltshire Record Office. These are all included in the card index at Dorset Record Office, although the records themselves are at Trowbridge.

Indexes to 1799 to all of these were published in BRS 53. The courts, with earliest dates for records (wills, admons and invs), are:

Peculiar of the Dean of Salisbury (this had jurisdiction over 28 Dorset parishes), from 1500.
Peculiar of the Dean and Chapter of Salisbury (included Stourpaine and Durweston in Dorset), 1604-1799
Chardstock, 1639-1799
Fordington and Writhlington, 1660-1799
Gillingham, 1658-1799
Lyme Regis and Halstock, 1664-1799
Netherbury in ecclesia, 1608-1799
Preston and Sutton Pointz, 1761-1799
Yetminster and Grimston, 1654-1799.

The Wiltshire Record Office has card or MS indexes to records of these courts to 1857.

For a map of Dorset and list of parishes in peculiars, see page 14.

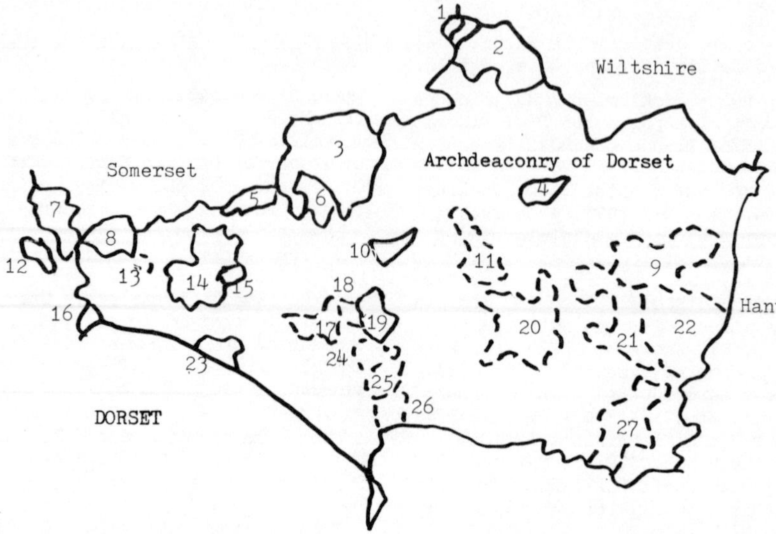

Parishes in Dorset in jurisdictions other than the archdeaconry of Dorset:

Note: records of the prebends of Chardstock, Lyme Regis and Halstock, Netherbury in ecclesia, Preston and Sutton Poyntz, and Yetminster and Grimston are to be found also in the peculiar court of the dean of Salisbury (in addition to the parishes in the direct jurisdiction of that court). Places in the liberty of Frampton also appear in the archdeaconry and consistory records.

BB : Burton Bradstock; C : Chardstock; CC : Corfe Castle; CP : Gt. Canford and Poole; DC : Dean and Chapter of Salisbury; DS : Dean of Salisbury; E : Diocese of Exeter; F : Frampton; FW : Fordington and Writhlington; G : Gillingham; LR : Lyme Regis and Halstock; MA : Milton Abbas; N : Netherbury; P : Preston and Sutton Poyntz; SM : Sturminster Marshall; ST : Stratton; WM : Wimborne Minster; Y : Yetminster and Grimston.

Alton Pancras DS10; Anderson DS20; Beaminster N&DS14; Bere Hacket DS3; Bere Regis DS20; Bettiscombe F13; Bincombe F25; Bloxworth DS20; Bourton G1; Burton Bradstock BB23; Gt Canford CP22; Castleton DS3; Caundle Marsh DS3; Chardstock C&DS7; Charminster DS19; Chetnole Y&DS6; Clifton Maybank DS3; Nether Compton DS3; Over Compton DS3; Compton Valence F17; Corfe Castle CC27; Corfe Mullen SM21; Dalwood (archd. of Dorset, detd.) 12; Folke DS3; Fordington FW24; Frampton F17; Gillingham G2; Grimston Y18; Halstock LR&DS5; Hamworthy SM21; Haydon DS3; Hermitage DS3; Holnest DS3; Kingston CC27; Leigh Y&DS6; Lillington DS3; Longburton DS3; Lyme Regis LR&DS16; Lytchett Minster SM21; Mapperton DS15; Milborne Stileham DS20; Milton Abbas MA11; Motcombe G2; Netherbury N&DS14; Oborne DS3; Poole CP22; Preston P26; Ryme Intrinsica DS3; Sherborne DS3; Stockland (archd. of Dorset, detd.) 12; Stockwood DS3; Stourpaine DC4; Stratton ST&DS18; Sturminster Marshall SM21; Sutton Poyntz P&DS26; Thorncombe E8; Thornford DS3; Tomson DS20; Turners Puddle DS20; Wambrook C&DS7; Wimborne Minster WM9; Winterborne Came F25; Winterborne Herringstone F25; Winterborne Kingston DS20; Winterborne Tomson DS20; Woolland MA11; North Wootton DS3; Yetminster Y&DS6.

Durham and Northumberland

(border area between counties incl. Newcastle now in Tyne and Wear; south-east border of co.Durham now in Cleveland)

Since 1858: Probate records for England and Wales are at the Principal Registry of the Family Division, Somerset House, Strand, London WC2R 1LP. Indexes to these are held locally at the Newcastle

Durham and **Northumberland** continued

District Probate Registry, Plummer House, Croft Street, Newcastle upon Tyne NE1 6NP, tel. 0632 28543; for other copies, see page 1.

Registered copy wills proved at Newcastle, 1858-1941 (from 1926 also incl. Gateshead and places immediately south of the River Tyne) are deposited at the Northumberland Record Office; those proved at Durham, 1858-1940 (for co. Durham) are deposited at the Dept. of Palaeography, University of Durham.

Before 1858: County Durham and most of Northumberland were in the diocese of Durham in the province of York. For records of P.C.Y., see page 46; and see also records of P.C.C., page 2.

Apart from P.C.Y. and P.C.C., nearly all probate records for both counties are housed by the

Dept. of Palaeography and Diplomatic, University of Durham, 5 The College, Durham DH1 3EQ (0385 61478)

(no special readers' ticket required). The **Consistory Court of Durham** covered all of both counties (except for a peculiar, below). There are card indexes to wills, admons, invs 1540-1616 (superseding the printed index 1540-99 (Newcastle upon Tyne Records Committee Publication 8) and the TS index 1540-1812 by J.W. Robinson, at SofG and Newcastle upon Tyne Ref. Library) and 1832-1857. The intervening period 1617-1831 is covered by older MS calendars.

The only other probate records for the counties are at the Borthwick Institute, York (see page 46).

Peculiar of the Archbishop of York in Hexham and Hexhamshire (until 1837 only: Hexham with Whitley; Allendale with West Allen, St Peter's Allenheads and Ninebanks; St John Lee with St Oswald's and St Mary Bingfield; all in Northumberland).

Printed index: probate act book, 1593-1602 (260 only)(Yorks. Arch. Soc. R.S. 60, pp.184-89). After 1660 records of the court are merged with P.C.Y., page 46; also some wills and invs, 1694-1706, at Northumberland Record Office, index in "J.N'hmbd.& Durham FHS" **6**, 2 (Jan.81); and the

Prebend of Tockerington (jurisdiction: Thockrington in Northumberland).

A few records, 1741-1744.

For a map, see page 46.

Essex

(partly now in Greater London)

Since 1858: Probate records for England and Wales are at the Principal Registry of the Family Division, Somerset House, Strand, London WC2R 1LP. For copies of printed indexes elsewhere see page 1.

Registered copy wills proved at Ipswich, 1858-1941 (for north Essex only, to 1926) are deposited locally at the Ipswich branch of the Suffolk Record Office, and are indexed.

Before 1858: Essex was in the province of Canterbury and diocese of London. For P.C.C. see page 2. Abstracts of all Essex wills in P.C.C. 1558-1603 (339) are published in "Elizabethan Life" vol. 4 "Wills of Essex Gentry and Merchants". Apart from P.C.C. most of the probate records for the county are held at

Essex Record Office, Chelmsford (0245 267222 ext 2104).

There is a published index to all wills at the Office, for all courts in one sequence, 1400-1619, 1620-1720, 1721-1857 (BRS 78,79,84), which covers almost the whole county. These comprise the **Archdeaconries of Colchester** (from 1500), **Essex** (from 1400) and **Middlesex** (Essex & Herts div; from 1554), and **Bishop of London's Commissary** (Essex & Herts div; from 1483), as well as the **Peculiars of Writtle with Roxwell** (from 1607), **Good Easter** (from 1613), **Bocking** (post-1620) and the **Sokens** (post-1620; in BRS 79 these are listed out of place, pages vii-viii).

Abstracts of 278 wills from these courts, 1558-1603, are published in "Elizabethan Life" vol. 5 "Wills of Essex Gentry and Yeomen"; abstracts of all the remainder for the three Archdeaconry Courts (only; the Commissary Court and the Peculiars are not included) are published in "Essex Wills", vol.1, 1558-1565 (1,002), vol.2, 1565-71 (880), vol.3, 1571-77 (1,050); vols.4-7, 1577-1603, in preparation.

Admons are calendared separately (MS only) and commence: **Commissary Court of London** 1619; **Archdeaconries of Colchester** 1663; **Essex** 1559; **Middlesex** 1660; Peculiars of: **Bocking** 1665; **Good Easter** 1613; **Sokens** 1632; **Writtle** 1637.

Invs for the **Peculiar of Writtle** are published in "Farm and Cottage Inventories" by F.W. Steer (C17-18, 250).

Essex continued

Some Essex probate records are also to be found at the Greater London Record Office, 40 Northampton Road, London EC1R 0AB, in the **Consistory Court of London.** At present there are only MS calendars, 1514-1669 (a few earlier) to wills and chronological lists to wills 1669-1857, admons 1540-1857; but a full index to wills, 1492-1719, in in preparation for publication by BRS.

Exceptions:

Guildhall Library, London EC2P 2EJ, holds records of the **London Division of the Commissary Court of London,** which includes places in Essex on the outskirts of London: Chingford, Epping, Leyton, Loughton, Nazeing, Waltham Holy Cross, Walthamstow and Woodford. Published index, wills and admons 1374-1570 (BRS 82,86; 1571-1625 in press, 1626-1700 waiting publication). MS calendar only to unpublished period to 1857. Abstracts of Essex wills, 1558-1603 (418) published in "Elizabethan Wills of South-West Essex".

The Guildhall Library, London, also holds records of the **Peculiar of the Dean and Chapter of St Paul's,** which includes places scattered throughout Essex: Barling, Belchamp St Pauls, Heybridge, Navestock, Tillingham, and Wickham St Pauls.
Index (MS, 19th cent.) wills 1535-1672; calendar only, wills 1672-1840, admons 1646-1837. Full index in preparation for publication by BRS.

Probate records of St Mary Maldon are at the City of Westminster Archives Dept., Victoria Library, Buckingham Palace Road, London SW1W 9UD in the **Royal Peculiar of the Dean and Chapter of Westminster.** For records and indexes, see page 26.

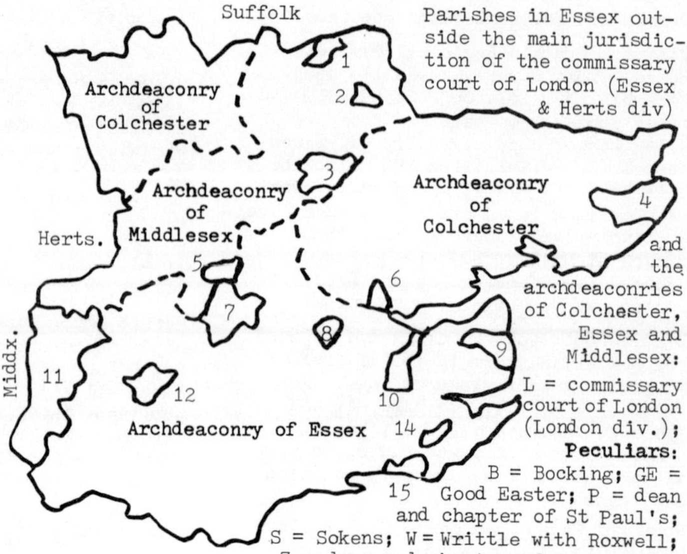

Parishes in Essex outside the main jurisdiction of the commissary court of London (Essex & Herts div) and the archdeaconries of Colchester, Essex and Middlesex: L = commissary court of London (London div.); **Peculiars:** B = Bocking; GE = Good Easter; P = dean and chapter of St Paul's; S = Sokens; W = Writtle with Roxwell; Z = dean and chapter of Westminster (not marked on map).

Barling P14; Belchamp St Pauls P1; Bocking B3; Borley B; Chingford L11; Chrishall Z; Little Coggeshall B; Good Easter GE5 & Z; Epping L11; Heybridge P6; Kirkby-le-Soken S4; Latchingdon B10; Leyton L11; Loughton L11; Maldon St Mary Z; Milton in Prittlewell B15; Navestock P12; Nazeing L11; Newport Z; Roxwell W7; Runsell in Danbury B8; Southchurch B15; Stisted B3; Thorpe-le-Soken S4; Tillingham P9; Waltham Holy Cross L11; Walthamstow L11; Walton-le-Soken S4; Wickham St Pauls P2; Woodford L11; Writtle W7.

Gloucestershire and Bristol

(Southern Glos. and Bristol now in Avon)

Since 1858: Probate records for England and Wales are at the Principal Registry of the Family Division, Somerset House, Strand, London WC2R 1LP. Indexes to these are held locally at the Gloucestershire Record Office (to 1929) and the Bristol Record Office (to 1900).

Registered copy wills proved at Gloucester, 1858-1941 (to 1926, Glos. only, excl. Bristol) are deposited at the Gloucestershire Record Office, and are indexed to 1931. Registered copy wills proved at Bristol, 1858-1941 (Bristol and Bath County Court districts to 1926)

Gloucestershire and **Bristol** continued

are deposited at the Bristol Record Office. Original wills proved at Bristol are still at the Bristol District Probate Registry, Ground Floor, Sperry House, Temple Back, Bristol BS1 6EP, tel. 0272 23915, but 7 days notice is required for pre-1929 wills.

Before 1858: Gloucestershire and the city of Bristol were in the province of Canterbury. Most of the **county** was in the diocese of Gloucester, but the **city of Bristol**, comprising 17 parishes, and several neighbouring parishes in Gloucestershire, were in the diocese of Bristol; and also 4 Somerset parishes.

Most probate records for the **county**, apart from P.C.C. (see page 2) are at

Gloucestershire Record Office
(0452 425295)(daily charge)

which publishes a full guide in "Gloucestershire Family History"(£1.50). Apart from the Bristol area virtually the whole county is covered by the **Consistory Court of Gloucester**, for which there are published indexes to wills, 1541-1650 (BRS 12) and to wills 1660-1800 and admons 1684-1800 (BRS 34). MS indexes to 1857.

"Wills proved in Gloucestershire Peculiar Courts" indexes probate records (also at the Glos. R.O.) for **Peculiars of Bibury** (incl. Aldsworth, Barnsley and Winson) 1619-1833; **Bishops Cleeve** (and Stoke Orchard) 1622-1765; and **Withington** (and Dowdeswell) 1624-1776. Partial indexes also in BRS 12; and see Consistory.

The Glos. R.O. has TS indexes to two collections of miscellaneous wills and invs, pre-1858, found at the probate registry, not included in the printed calendars.

Bristol Record Office
(0272 266031 ext 442)

holds probate records for Bristol and neighbouring Gloucestershire parishes (listed right) which were covered by the **Consistory Court of the Bishop of Bristol in the Deanery of Bristol.** There is a printed index to wills 1568-1792 and admons 1770-1793 (BRS 17); MS calendars to wills and admons to 1857; admons 1661-1769 (index in progress); invs 1609-1767 (indexed). Published: Bristol wills 1546-1593, 1597-1598, 2 vols. TS reproduction; Clifton and Westbury probate invs, 1609-1761 (Bristol University, 1981).

Another source for Bristol wills is in the Bristol Great Orphan Books (also at Bristol R.O.), also indexed in BRS 17.

See also the "Guide to the Bristol Archives Office" and the "Diocese of Bristol: a catalogue of the records of the Bishop and Archdeacons and of the Dean and Chapter" (1970).

Places in the jurisdiction of the **Consistory Court of Bristol:**

All parishes in the city of Bristol; the Gloucestershire parishes of: Almondesbury, Alveston, Clifton, Compton Greenfield, Elberton, Filton, Henbury, Horfield, St George Bristol, Littleton-on-Severn, Mangotsfield, Olveston, Stapleton, Stoke Gifford, Westbury -on-Trym, Winterbourne St Michael; and Abbots Leigh (Som.); Bedminster (Som.)(from 1845 only).

Peculiar of Bibury, 3
Aldsworth, Barnsley, Bibury, Winson

Peculiar of Bishops Cleeve, 1
Bishops Cleeve, Stoke Orchard

Peculiar of Withington, 2
Dowdeswell, Withington

Note. The detached parish of Shenington, formerly in Glos., was in that diocese until 1837 when it was transferred to the diocese of Worcester.

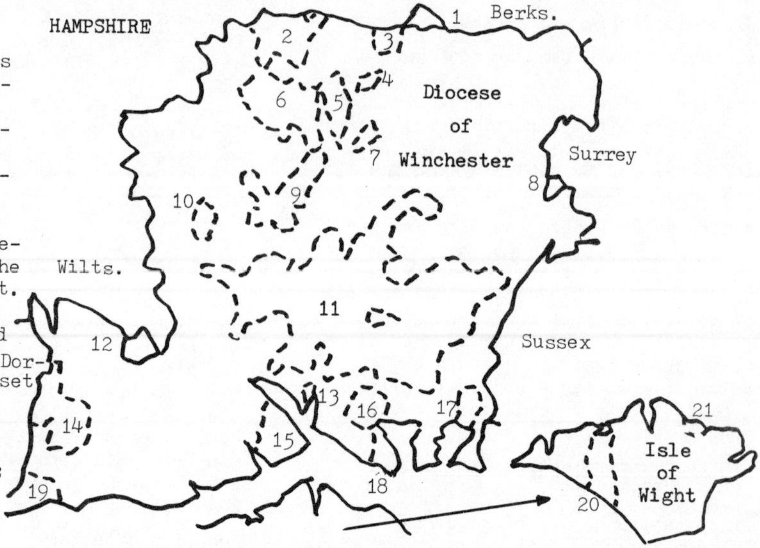

Hampshire parishes and places in peculiars. In area '11' unless otherwise indicated. All were also subject to the consistory court and most are also likely to appear in the archdeaconry court.

Allington; New and Old Alresford; Alverstoke 18; Ashmansworth 2; North Baddesley; Baughurst 3; Binstead (IoW) 21; Bishopstoke; Bishops Waltham; Braishfield; Brambridge; Bramshaw (diocese of Salisbury) 12; Brickmerston 15; Brighstone (IoW) 20; Brockhmapton 17; Burghclere 2; Bursash 15; Bursledon 13; Cadlands 15; Calbourne (IoW) 20; Catisfield 16; Charlecott 6; Cheriton; Chilbolton 9; Chilcombe; Combe (nr Petersfield); Compton; Cranborne 9; Crawley 9; Dean (nr Fareham) 16; Denmead; Droxford; Durley; Easton; Exbury 15; Exton; Fareham 16; Fawley 15; Freefolk 6; Frensham (arch. of Surrey) 8; Froxfield; Gosport 18; Hamble 13; Hambledon; Hannington 4; Harbridge 14; Hardley 15; Havant 17; Highclere 2; Hill; Hoe; Holbury 15; Holdenhurst 19; Houghton 10; Hunton 9; Hursley; Hurstbourne Priors 6; Hythe 15; Kilmeston; Langley 15; Leigh 17; Lepe 15; Littleton 9; Medstead; Meonstoke; East and West Meon; Merdon; Michelmersh; Midlington; Morestead; Newtown (IoW); Otterbourne; Overton 5; Ovington; Ower 15; Owslebury; Oxenbourne; Polhampton 5; Privett; Ramsdean; Ringwood 14; St Mary Bourne 6; Shamblehurst; Shedfield; Silkstead; Soberton; Stanswood 15; Steep; Stone 15; South Stoneham; Stratfield Mortimer (archd. of Berks, dioc. of Salisbury) 1; Sutton Scotney 9; Swanmore; Tadley 3; Tichborne; Twyford; Upham; Bishops Waltham; North Waltham 7; Warnford; Whitchurch 6; Winchester St Cross or St Faith; Winnall; Wonston 9; East Woodhay 2.

Hampshire and Isle of Wight

(Bournemouth area now in Dorset; Isle of Wight now a separate county)

Since 1858: Probate records for England and Wales are at the Principal Registry of the Family Division, Somerset House, Strand, London WC2R 1LP. Indexes to these to 1928 are held locally at the Hampshire Record Office, Winchester; for other copies, see page 1.

Registered copy wills proved at Winchester, 1858-1941 (to 1926 for Hampshire only) are deposited at the Hampshire Record Office and are partially indexed.

Before 1858: Hampshire (including the Isle of Wight) was in the province of Canterbury and diocese of Winceshter.

Apart from P.C.C. (see page 2 and right), all probate records for the county are at the

Hampshire Record Office, 20 Southgate St, Winchester SO23 9EF (0962 63153)

which issues "Wills in the Hampshire Record Office" (10p + postage).

There are the following indexes to cover the four main series of records (Consistory Court wills, Archdeaconry of Winchester Court wills, Peculiar Courts wills, Consistory Court admons):

1. **Pre-1570**. All wills. Personal and place names, occupations, TS.

Hampshire continued

2. **1571-1659**. All wills and admons. Personal and place names, occupations. Computer-based, print-out and microfiche available from late 1986.
3. **1660-1857**. All wills. Card index.
4. **1660-1671**. Admons. Card index.
5. **1672-1857**. Admons. TS calandar arranged year by year under initial letter of surname, copied from contemporary finding aids.

Printed index: "Wills, Administrations and Inventories with the Winchester Diocesan Records", A.J. Willis, 1968. This is of a small collection, now at the Hampshire R.O., mainly Consistory (1617-1640) and Archdeaconry (1617-1626).

TS copies of calendars, Consistory wills 1502-1857, Archdeaconry wills 1502-1792; also MS list of Hampshire wills in P.C.C. 1671-1734, by H.A. Pitman; all at Soc. of Genealogists.

Herefordshire

(now part of Hereford and Worcester)

Since 1858: Probate records for England and Wales are at the Principal Registry of the Family Division, Somerset House, Strand, London WC2R 1LP. Indexes to these (to 1929) are held locally at the Glos. Record Office; see also page 1.

Registered copy wills proved at Hereford (for Herefordshire), 1858-1928, are deposited at the National Library of Wales, Aberystwyth, and are indexed.

Before 1858: Herefordshire was in the province of Canterbury and diocese of Hereford.

Apart from P.C.C. (page 2) probate records for most of the county are at the

Record Office, Harold Street, Hereford (0432 265441)

The main collections are for the **Episcopal Consistory Court of Hereford**, which covered most of the county, and the **Consistory Court of the Dean of Hereford**, which included Hereford itself and 25 nearby parishes (listed right). Card index to wills in both courts, 1600-1660. Chronological list to Epis-Consistory Court wills and invs 1539-99, invs 1628-1641. After 1660, to 1857, indexes in act books to wills and admons for both courts.

Also, three peculiars:
Little Hereford (Heref.) and **Ashford Carbonell** (Salop.), from 1662;
Upper Bullinghope or **Bullingham**, from 1675; **Moreton Magna** or **Moreton on Lugg**, from 1668 (all indexed).

A consolidated index to all records in the two consistory courts and three peculiars to 1700 is in preparation for publication by the BRS.

Eight parishes in the S-W of the county were in the **Archdeaconry of Brecon** (diocese of St David's). Records at the National Library of Wales, page 57.

Parishes in the **Consistory of the Dean of Hereford** (D):
Allensmore; Blakemore; Breinton; Brockhampton 7; Canon Pyon 2; Clehonger; Dewsall 8; Dinedor; Eaton Bishop; Hampton Bishop; **Hereford**; Holmer; Huntingdon; Kingstone; Madley; Mardon; Moreton Jeffreys 3; Norton Canon 4; Pipe; Preston on Wye; Preston Wynne; Putley 7; Thruxton; Tyberton; Withington; Woolhope 7.

Archdeaconry of Brecon (B):
Clodock; Dulas; Michaelchurch Escley; Ewyas Harold; Llancillo; St Margaret; Rowlston; Walterstone; Fwddog, 9.

Peculiars:
Little Hereford 1; Moreton on Lugg 5; Bullingham 6.

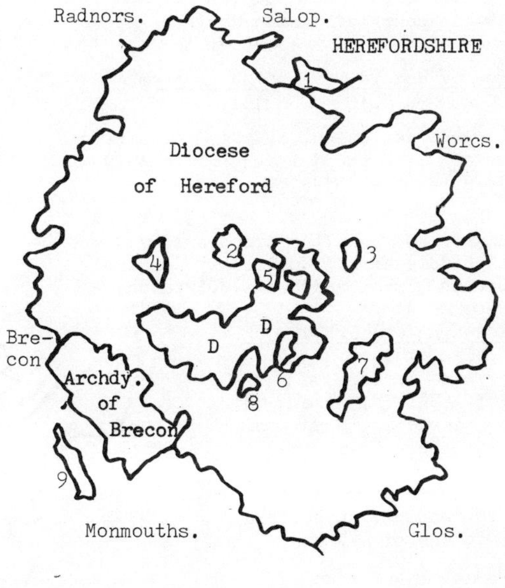

Hertfordshire

Since 1858: Probate records for England and Wales are at the Principal Registry of the Family Division, Somerset House, Strand, London WC2R 1LP. In addition to Somerset House, a copy of the index is available locally at the Huntingdon branch of the Cambridgeshire Record Office. For other copies, see page 1.

Before 1858: Hertfordshire was in the province of Canterbury - for records of P.C.C., see page 2.

Apart from P.C.C., probate records for most of the county are at the

Hertfordshire Record Office, Hertford (0992 555105)

(see guide "Genealogical Sources").

Apart from parishes on the eastern border, the county was in the intermixed jurisdictions of the **Archdeaconry of St Albans** (diocese of London) (mainly SW corner) and the **Archdeaconry of Huntingdon (Hitchin Division)** (diocese of Lincoln). All probate records for these two courts are in a consolidated card index (St Albans, wills from 1415, admons from 1540; Huntingdon, wills from 1557, admons from 1610). Printed index to Archdeaconry of Huntingdon wills and admons in act books, 1566-1573, 1596-1599 (BRS 42, pp.210-16).

Until 1609, most records for the **Archdeaconry of Huntingdon** (the major part of the county) are at the

County Record Office, Huntingdon (Cambs. C.C.)(0480 52181 ext 42)

(see "Genealogical Sources in Cambridgeshire"). Printed index, wills 1479-1609, admons 1559-1609 (BRS 42).

Eastern border parishes (31 listed right), were in the **Archdeaconry Court of Middlesex and Commissary Court of London (Essex and Herts. Division)** records at

Essex Record Office, Chelmsford.

Printed indexes, wills 1431-1857 (BRS 78, 79 and 84).
MS calendars to admons, commissary from 1691; archdeaconry from 1660.

Archdeaconry of Bedford (diocese of Lincoln):

Caddington (1)
Studham (2)

The **Consistory Court of London** had concurrent jurisdiction with the Archdeaconries of St Albans and Middlesex, so some Herts. testators are to be found amongst the records of this court, at the Greater London Record Office (see page 26). Calendar from 1514, and index in preparation (to 1719) for publication by BRS.

The parishes of Albury, Brent Pelham and Furneux Pelham were in the **Peculiar of the Dean and Chapter of St Paul's**, records at the

Guildhall Library, London EC2P 2EJ (see page 26) wills 1560-1837 (card index to Herts testators at Herts R.O.), admons 1646-1837 (calendar). Full index in preparation for publication by BRS.

Places in the east of Hertfordshire in the jurisdiction of the Archdeaconry of Middlesex and Commissary Court of London (Essex and Herts. divisions)(diocese of London); and the Peculiar Court of the Dean and Chapter of St Paul's (**P**):

Albury (P); Gt Amwell; Anstey; Barkway; Barley; Braughing; Brent Pelham (P); Broxbourne; Buckland; Cheshunt; Eastwick; Furneux Pelham (P); Gilston; Much and Little Hadham; Hoddesden; Gt and Little Hormead; Hunsdon; Layston; Meesden; Reed; Royston; Sawbridgeworth; Standon; Stanstead Abbots; Stanstead St Margarets; Stocking Pelham; Bishops Stortford; Thorley; Thundridge; Ware; Widford; Wormley; Wyddial.

HERTFORDSHIRE

Huntingdonshire

(now part of Cambridgeshire)

See "Genealogical Sources in Cambridgeshire" by Michael Farrar, Cambridgeshire Record Offices, 1979, 95p.

Since 1858: Probate records for England and Wales are at the Principal Registry of the Family Division, Somerset House, Strand, London WC2R 1LP. Indexes to these (to 1934) are held locally at the County Record Office (Cambridgeshire C.C.), Huntingdon. For other copies, see page 1.

Registered copies of Huntingdonshire wills proved at Peterborough, 1858-1941 are at the Northamptonshire Record Office, Northampton, and are indexed.

Before 1858: Huntingdonshire was in the province of Canterbury and formed the Archdeaconry of Huntingdon in the diocese of Lincoln.

Apart from P.C.C. (see page 2) probate records for virtually the whole county are at the

<u>County Record Office, Huntingdon</u>
(part of Cambridgeshire Record Office)
(0480 52181 ext 42).

Except for a few places (see below) the county was entirely within the jurisdiction of the **Commissary Court of the Bishop of Lincoln and of the Archdeacon in the Archdeaconry of Huntingdon.** Printed index: wills 1479-1652, admons 1559-1614 (BRS 42). MS index, wills 1615-1857, admons 1662-1688; MS calendar, admons 1691-1857.

Peculiars:
Brampton 1549-1855; **Buckden** 1661-1855; **Stow Longa** (incl. Barham, Little Catworth, Easton and Spaldwick) 1661-1857; **Leighton Bromswold** 1738-1838.
Printed index: Trans. Cambs. & Hunts. Arch. Soc., 6, pt.3, pp.76-96. Buckden and Stow Longa are also partially indexed in BRS 57.

Exceptions:
Washingley, in the **Consistory Court of Peterborough**, see page 30.

Records for places in the Peculiars of Stow Longa and Leighton Bromswold may also be found in the **Peculiar Court of the Dean and Chapter of Lincoln**, see page 25.

Places outside the jurisdiction of the archdeaconry court:

Brampton (4); Buckden (5); Leighton Bromswold (2); Stow Longa with Little Catworth, Easton and Spaldwick (3); Washingley (1).

Kent

See "A Guide to Sources for Family History" (Kent County Archives Office)

Since 1858: Probate records for England and Wales are at the Principal Registry of the Family Division, Somerset House, Strand, London WC2R 1LP. Indexes to these (over 50 years old) are held locally at the East Sussex Record Office, Lewes; for other copies see page 1.

Before 1858: Kent was in the province of Canterbury - for records of P.C.C. see page 2.

Apart from P.C.C., probate records for most of the county are at the

<u>Kent Archives Office, Maidstone</u>
(0622 671411 ext 3363)

The county comprised the two dioceses of Canterbury and Rochester.

Eastern Kent was in the diocese of Canterbury. Jurisdiction of consistory and archdeaconry courts was intermingled and overlapping, so indexes to both courts should be examined.
Printed indexes: wills and admons 1396-1577 (BRS 50, 65); 1640-1650 (BRS 50).
Calendars (separate for each court), wills and admons 1578-1857 (indexing in progress for publication by BRS).

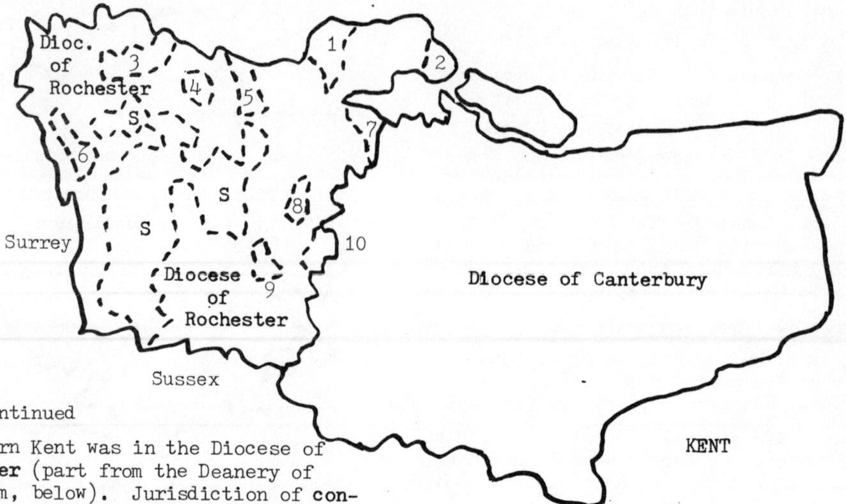

Kent continued

Western Kent was in the Diocese of **Rochester** (part from the Deanery of Shoreham, below). Jurisdiction of **consistory** and **archdeaconry** courts was concurrent. Printed index: wills and admons 1440-1561 (Kent A.S.9)(Consistory only). Consolidated card index, wills only, to both courts, 1498-1857 (noticeable decline in business from c1750). Calendars to admons from 1562.

38 parishes in western Kent were in the **Peculiar of the Deanery of Shoreham.** Original records are now at the Lambeth Palace Library, London SE1 7JU, but the Kent A.O. has all these on microfilm. Indexes: wills and admons 1614-1821, 1841 (C19 calendar; also TS index at SG). Later records appear to be missing.

Peculiar of Cliffe (that parish only). Index: all records 1671-1845. See also Rochester card index.

After 1846 records for the parishes of Charlton, Deptford, Eltham, Greenwich, Lee, Lewisham, Plumstead and Woolwich should be found in the **Consistory Court of London** at the Greater London R.O.

Peculiar Deanery of Shoreham (S):

Bexley 3; Brasted; Chevening; Chiddingstone; St Mary Cray; Crayford 3; Darenth 4; Downe 6; Eynsford; East Farleigh 10; Farningham; Gillingham 7; Grain 2; Halstead; Hayes; Hever; Hunton 10; Ide Hill; Ifield; Ightham; Keston 6; Knockholt; Lidsing; East Malling 8; Meopham; Northfleet 5; Orpington; Otford; East Peckham 9; Penshurst; Plaxtol; Sevenoaks; Shoreham; Stansted; Sundridge; Wrotham.

Peculiar of Cliffe (at Hoo) - 1.

Lancashire

(now split between the counties of Lancashire, Greater Manchester and Merseyside; Furness now in Cumbria and southern border area in Cheshire)

See "Handlist of Genealogical Sources", Lancashire R.O., 1983 (£2.50 + 45p p&p).

Since 1858: Probate records for England and Wales are at the Principal Registry of the Family Division, Somerset House, Strand, London WC2R 1LP. Indexes to these are held locally by the Lancashire Record Office, Preston (to 1928); the Liverpool Record Office (to 1928); and the Greater Manchester Record Office, 56 Marshall Street, New Cross, Ancoats, Manchester M4 5FU (061 247 3383). For other copies, see page 1.

Registered copy wills proved at Lancaster, 1858-1940 (until 1926 confined to Lancashire excl. Manchester, Salford and Hundred of West Derby) and Liverpool (Hundred of West Derby)(many damaged), 1858-1940, are deposited at the Lancashire Record Office, Preston.

Before 1858: Lancashire was in the province of York - for records of P.C.Y., see page 46; and also records of P.C.C. page 2. Printed index: Lancs. wills and admons in P.C.C., 1650-1660 (Lancs & Ches R.S. 4, pp. 250-300).

Lancashire continued

Apart from P.C.Y. and P.C.C., nearly all probate records for the county are held at the

Lancashire Record Office, Preston (0772 54868)

The county was in the diocese of Chester, but records for the archdeaconry of Richmond (north of the Ribble) are generally separate.

For the **Consistory Court of Chester** there are indexes published by Lancs. and Cheshire Record Soc. to wills and admons, 1545-1837, with the prospect of further volumes to come.

Meanwhile there is a card index to the remaining years, 1838-1857 (A-G also in typescript).

In this diocese only, estates worth less than £40 were kept in a separate 'infra' series, and in the published index volumes are in a separate volume before 1665, and in appendices from 1660 to 1800. Since 1800 they have been indexed jointly with the main series. To 1820 Cheshire and Lancashire wills and admons are intermingled, but from 1821 they are in separate sections in each volume.

Lancs & Ches Rec Soc vols and dates:
1545-1650 (main series) 2 and 4;
1590-1665 ('infra' series) 52;
1660-1800 15,18,20,22,25,37,38,44,45;
1801-1820 62,63,78;
1821-1837 (Lancs separate) 107,113, 118,120.

Vols 33,43,52 list miscellaneous wills 1487-1800; and additional wills and admons for 1670 and 1692 are in vol 63.

The county north of the River Ribble lay in the **Archdeaconry of Richmond (Western Deaneries)**. The Lancs and Ches Record Soc has published indexes to **all** the Lancashire records 1457-1857 vols 10,13,23,66,99 and 105.

Manorial Court of Halton (parish of Halton only). Printed index: wills and admons 1615-1815, L&CRS 23,66,99.

In addition to P.C.Y. (above) there are a few Lancashire wills at the

Borthwick Institute, York

for Aighton, Chaigley and Bailey, in the **Exchequer Court of York** (page 46), and for Broughton, Kirkby Ireleth and Seathwaite (Furness) in the **Peculiar Court of the Dean and Chapter of York** and occasionally in the **Chancery Court of York** (page 46).

Rochdale Public Library has a big collection of abstracts of wills and admons relating to Rochdale people, 1553-1810.

Peculiar of Dean and Chapter of York (1): Broughton, Kirkby Ireleth, Seathwaite.

Manor of Halton (2)

Diocese of York (3): Aighton, Bailey, Chaigley

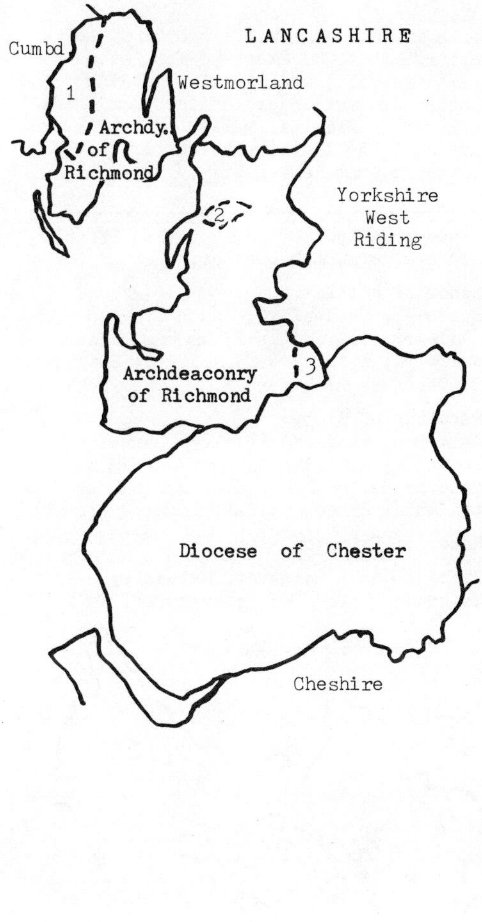

Leicestershire

Since 1858: Probate records for England and Wales are at the Principal Registry of the Family Division, Somerset House, Strand, London WC2R 1LP. Indexes to these held locally in Leicester will be transferred over a period from the District Probate Registry, Government Buildings, Newarke St., Leicester, to the Leicestershire Record Office. There is also a set at the Nottinghamshire Record Office. For other copies, see page 1.

Registered copy wills proved at Leicester, 1858-1940 (to 1926 for Leicestershire only) are deposited at the Leicestershire Record Office (card index to 1918). Original wills, 1858-1969, are still held at the Leicester District Probate Registry.

Places outside the jurisdiction of the archdeaconry of Leicester:

Manor of Rothley:
Barsby 3; Chadwell 1; South Croxton 3; Gaddesby 3; Grimston 2; Keyham 8; Mountsorrel 4; Rothley 4; Saxelby 2; Somerby 5; Wartnaby 2; Wycomb 1.

Peculiar of Groby:
Anstey 6; Bradgate Park 6; Charnwood Forest 6; Cropston 6; Glenfield 6; Hallgate 6; Newton Linford 6; Ratby 6; Swanton under Bardon 7; Swithland 6

Manor of Evington - 6

Prebend of St Margaret, Leicester - 10: Knighton; Leicester St Margaret.

Archdeaconry of Leicester

Before 1858: Leicestershire was in the province of Canterbury and formed the archdeaconry of Leicester in the diocese of Lincoln.

Apart from P.C.C. (see page 2) all probate records for the county are at

Leicestershire Record Office, Leicester
(0533 554100 ext 238)

which issues an information sheet (no.5) "How to Trace your Family".

For the **Archdeaconry of Leicester** there are printed indexes to wills, 1495-1750, and admons, 1556-1750 (BRS 27, 51) and a consolidated card index to all records, 1751-1857.

BRS 27 and 51 also print indexes to the four peculiars
St Margaret in Leicester: 1543-1800
Manor of Rothley: 1575-1800
Manor of Evington: 1581-1800
Peculiar of Groby: 1580, 1636-1637, 1670-1800.

Wills and admons for 1801-1857 are included in the main card index.

The R.O. also has a large collection of Leicester will abstracts, 1563-1800.

Lincolnshire

(northern border now in Humberside)

Since 1858: Probate records for England and Wales are at the Principal Registry of the Family Division, Somerset House, Strand, London WC2R 1LP. Indexes to these are at present held locally at the Lincoln Probate Sub-Registry, Mill House, Brayford Side North, Lincoln, though there is a possibility those over 50 years old may be transferred in due course to the Lincolnshire Archives Office. For other copies, see page 1.

Registered copy wills proved at Lincoln (for Lincolnshire), 1858-1941, are deposited at the Lincolnshire Archives Office, indexed to 1874 only. Original wills are at Lincoln Probate Sub-Registry.

Before 1858: Lincolnshire was in the province of Canterbury and diocese of Lincoln. Nevertheless see also P.C.Y. (right and pages 46-47).

Apart from P.C.C. (see page 2) and P.C.Y., probate records for the whole county are at the

Lincolnshire Archives Office, Lincoln
(0522 25158)

which issues a leaflet on records for the family historian.

Lincolnshire continued

Most of the county was in the jurisdiction of the **Consistory Court of Lincoln** (the whole county from 1834). There are printed indexes to wills 1506-1653 (BRS 28,41) and admons 1540-1659 (BRS 52); a typed index to wills 1660-1750, and MS calendars to wills 1751-1857, admons 1660-1857; invs 1504-1831.

Until 1834 the **Archdeaconry of Stow** had separate jurisdiction over 78 parishes in the N-W of the county. There is a printed index to wills 1530-1699 and admons 1580-1699 in BRS 57; and MS calendars 1700-1834; MS list of invs 1616-1787.

There are printed indexes to wills, admons and invs for the complete period for all **Peculiars** in the county in BRS 57. Of these the **Peculiar of the Dean and Chapter of Lincoln** includes 25 parishes (1534-1834). The others are **Caistor** (1636-1833), **Corringham** (1632-1833), **Heydour** (1669-1836), **Kirton-in-Lindsey** (1535-1834), **Louth** (1612-1857), **Bishop Norton** (1613-1814), **Sleaford** (1610-1834) and **Stow in Lindsey** (1549-1833). Records for all except Louth became merged with the Consistory from about 1834.

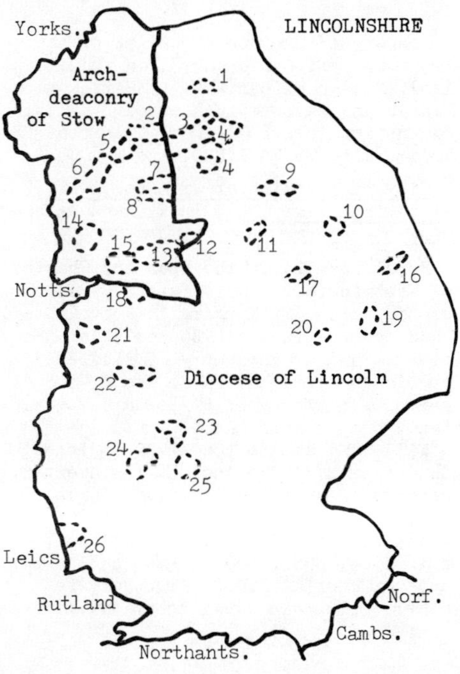

The <u>Soc of Gen</u> has a TS index to Lincs. wills and admons 1731-1857 in P.C.York.

Will abstracts, 1271-1532, published in Lincoln Record Soc. vols. 5,10,24.

Parishes and places not in the direct jurisdiction of the consistory court, i.e., in the archdeaconry of Stow or in one of the following peculiars: **Dean and Chapter of Lincoln** (D); **Caistor** (CA); **Corringham** (CO); **Heydour** (H); **Kirton in Lindsey** (K); **Louth** (L); **Bishop Norton** (BN); **Sleaford** or Lafford (SL); and **Stow in Lindsey** (ST).

Aisby in Corringham CO6; Aisby in Heydour H24; Aisthorpe, Alkborough; Althorpe; Appleby; Asgarby D20; Atterby BN7; Audleby CA4; Barlings; Belton in Axholme; Binbrook D9; Blyborough; Blyton; Bottesford; Bransby ST14; Brattleby; Broughton; Broxholme; Burton by Lincoln; Burton on Stather; Buslingthorpe; Caenby; Caistor CA4; Cammeringham; North and South Carlton D15; Cherry Willingham; Clixby CA4; Coates; Cold Hanworth; Corringham CO6; Crowle; Culverthorpe H24; Dalby D19; Dunholme D13; Dunstall CO6; Epworth; Faldingworth; Fenton; Fillingham; East Firsby; Fiskerton; Flixborough; Fonaby CA4; Friesthorpe D12; Frodingham; Gainsborough; Glentham D8; Glentworth; Grayingham; Greetwell; Hackthorne; Hainton D11; West Halton; Harpswell; Haxey; Heapham; Hemswell; Heydour H24; Hibaldstow D2; Holdingham SL23; Holton le Moor CA4; Huckerby CO6; Hundon CA4; Ingham; Kelby H24; North Kelsey D3; Kettlethorpe; Kirton in Lindsey K5; Knaith; Laughton; Lea; Lincoln St John, St Margaret, St Mary Magd. and St Nicholas D18; Louth L10; Luddington; Manton, Marton; Melton Ross D1; Messingham; Nettleham; Newton on Trent; Normanby; Normanby by Stow ST14; Northorpe CO6; Bishop Norton BN7; Oasby H24; Owmby by Spital; Owston; Redbourne; Reepham; Roxby with Risby; Saxby St Helen; Saxilby; Scamblesby D17; Scampton; Scawby; Scothorne; Scotter; Scotton; Scredington D25; Searby cum Owmby D3; Skillington D26; Sleaford SL23; Snarford; Snitterby; Somerby CO6; Southrey in p.Bardney D; Spital in the Street BN7; Spridlington; Springthorpe; Stow in Lindsey ST14; Strubby D16; Sturton ST14; Sudbrooke; Thurlby D21; Torksey; Upton; Waddingham; Wellingore D22; Welton by Lincoln D13; Whitton; Willingham; Willoughton; Winteringham; Winterton; Wroot; Yawthorpe CO6.

London and Middlesex

Since 1858: Probate records for England and Wales are at the Principal Registry of the Family Division, Somerset House, Strand, London WC2R 1LP. For copies of the printed index elsewhere, see page 1.

Before 1858: The city of London and county of Middlesex were in the province of Canterbury and diocese of London. The various jurisdictions are probably more complicated than anywhere else in the country and the searcher is advised to examine all major courts, split though they are between several record offices.

Greater London Record Office, 40 Northampton Road, London EC1R 0AB (01-633 6851).

Consistory Court of London. The superior court, with jurisdiction over the whole city and county except peculiars, so it should always be searched in addition to others listed below. Indexes are in preparation for publication by BRS, 1492-1719, meanwhile calendars, partly 19th cent, remain in use, 1492, 1508, 1514-1857.

Archdeaconry of Middlesex (Middlesex Division). Jurisdiction over 26 parishes in Middlesex (see list, right). Wills, 1608-1612, 1662-1701, admons 1667-1701 (19th cent MS calendar; full index in preparation for publication by BRS); wills 1702-1736 (card index, and in progress); wills 1737-1794, 1799, admons 1702-1760 (19th cent MS calendar); invs 1667-1773 (card index).

Guildhall Library, Aldermanbury, London EC2P 2EJ (01-606 3030)

See "Guide to the London Collections" 1978; and "A Guide to Genealogical Sources in the Guildhall Library" 2nd edn.

Commissary Court of London (London Division). Jurisdiction over about half the parishes both in the city and in the county. Printed index, wills and admons 1374-1625 (BRS 82, 86, 97) (1626-1700 for publication by BRS). Wills and admons 1571-1629 (modern MS index in short periods); 1629-1857 (MS calendar).

Archdeaconry of London. Jurisdiction over about 40 parishes in the city and 5 populous parishes bordering it; incl. St Botolph Aldgate, to which many mariners, dying abroad, were ascribed as residents (otherwise see P.C.C.).

Archdeaconry of London. Printed index, wills 1393-1421, 1524-1649, 1661-1700, admons 1564-1649, 1661-1700 (BRS 89,98). Wills and admons 1701-1781 (a few to 1807)(19th cent calendar)

Peculiar of the Dean and Chapter of St Paul's Cathedral. Jurisdiction over 4 parishes in the city and all or parts of 10 in the county. Wills 1535-1672 (MS 19th cent index); wills 1672-1837, admons 1646-1837 (calendars). New index in preparation for publication by BRS.

Royal Peculiar of St Katherine by the Tower. Wills 1689-1772, 1818, admons 1688-1793 (TS, for publication by BRS).

Corporation of London Record Office, Guildhall, London EC2P 2EJ.

Court of Husting. The court of the corporation of the city of London, with jurisdiction in the city and liberties, to 1688 only. Printed index and abstracts, wills 1258-1688 ("Calendar of Wills ... in the Court of Husting", R.R. Sharpe, 2 vols, 1888-9).

Lambeth Palace Library, London SE1 7JU (01-928 6222)

Deanery of the Arches (Peculiar of the Archbishop of Canterbury). Jurisdiction in thirteen city parishes (only). Wills, admons and invs, 1620-1780, 1832 (BRS 98).

Deanery of Croydon (Peculiar of the Archbishop of Canterbury). Jurisdiction incl. Middlesex parishes of Harrow with Pinner and Hayes with Norwood. Wills, admons and invs 1602-1832 (19th cent MS index, also TS at P.R.O. and S of G).

City of Westminster Archives Dept., Victoria Library, 160 Buckingham Palace Road, London SW1W 9UD (01-798-2180).

Royal Peculiar of the Dean and Chapter of Westminster. Jurisdiction, precincts of the Abbey, St Margaret's Westminster, Paddington - from c.1700 see under consistory and archdeaconry of Middlesex; precincts of St Martin le Grand, and parts of parishes of St Leonard Foster Lane, and St Anne and St Agnes.

Wills and admons 1504-1700 (printed in "Indexes to the Ancient Testamentary Records of Westminster", A.M. Burke, 1919), also, as above, and to 1828/30 (very few in later period)(calendar, printed by HMSO, 1864, never published; another copy at P.R.O., but very few other copies are known to exist).

London and **Middlesex,** continued

The parishes and chapelries in the city of London and the county of Middlesex are listed below, with the jurisdiction(s) into which they fell indicated as follows:

C : Commissary of London (London division); **L** : Archdeaconry of London; **M** : Archdeaconry of Middlesex; **A** : Peculiar Deanery of the Arches; **D** : Peculiar Deanery of Croydon; **P** : Peculiar of the Dean and Chapter of St Paul's; **K** : Peculiar of St Katherine-by-the-Tower; **W** : Peculiar of the Dean and Chapter of Westminster; **S** : Archdeaconry Court of Surrey (diocese of Winchester) - parishes in Southwark were still in that county in 1858 (see page 39).

Numbers refer to the map.

This list is based, for the city, on that in Lewis's "Topographical Dictionary" published in 1831, and includes places that may have been chapelries within other parishes and subsequently became parishes in their own right. Parishes were in the city or its immediate vicinity unless otherwise stated.

Acton C3; St Alban Wood Street C; Allhallows Barking C; Allhallows the Great L; Allhallows Honey Lane C; Allhallows the Less L; Allhallows Lombard Street A; Allhallows Staining C; Allhallows London Wall and St Augustin Papey L; St Alphage London Wall L; St Andrew Holborn L13; St Andrew Hubbard C; St Andrew Undershaft with St Mary Axe C; St Andrew-by-the-Wardrobe L; St Anne and St Agnes Aldersgate with St John Zachary W & L; St Anne Blackfriars C; St Anne (Soho) Westminster M; St Antholin C; Ashford M19; St Augustine Watling Street L; Friern Barnet P2; St Bartholomew by the Exchange L; St Bartholomew the Great L; St Bartholomew the Less L; Bedfont M19; St Benet Fink C; St Benet Gracechurch C; St Benet Paul's Wharf C; St Benet Sherehog C; Bethnal Green, St Matthew C1; St Botolph Aldersgate L; St Botolph Aldgate L; St Botolph Billingsgate C; St Botolph without Bishopsgate C; Bow C; Brentford M19; St Bride, Fleet Street C; Bromley St Leonard C1; Chelsea M17; Chiswick P16; Christchurch Greyfriars Newgate Street L; Christchurch Southwark S; Christchurch Spitalfields C1; St Christopher le Stocks C; St Clement Danes M; St Clement Eastcheap C; Cowley M19; Cranford M19; St Dionis Backchurch A; West Drayton P9; St Dunstan in the East A; St Dunstan in the West C; Ealing C3; Edgware C1; Edmonton C1; St Edmund the King C; Enfield C1; St Ethelburga L; St Faith P; Feltham M19; Finchley C1; Fulham C3; St Gabriel Fenchurch C; St George Bloomsbury C12; St George Botolph Lane C; St George in the East C1; St George Hanover Square M17; St George the Martyr and St Andrew above Bars L13; St George Southwark S; St Giles Cripplegate P; St Giles in the Fields C12; St Gregory by St Paul's P; Greenford C3; Hackney C1; Monken Hadley or Hadleigh C1; Hammersmith C3; Hampstead C1; Hampton M19; Hanwell M19; Hanworth C20; Harefield C3; Harlington M19; Harmondsworth M19; Harrow D4; Hayes D10; St Helen Bishopsgate P; Hendon C1; Heston M19; Highgate P6; Hillingdon M19; Hornsey C1; Hounslow M19; Hoxton (Shoreditch) P; Ickenham C3; Isleworth M19; Islington C1; St James Clerkenwell L13; St James Duke's Place C; St James (Piccadilly) Westminster M; St John Baptist L; St John Baptist Savoy L; St John Clerkenwell L13; St John Evangelist Watling Street A; St John Evangelist Westminster W18; St John Horsleydown S; St John Millbank (Smith Square) C; St John Zachary L; St Katherine Coleman L;

St Katherine Creechurch C; St Katherine by the Tower K; Kensington M17; Kingsbury C1; Laleham M19; St Lawrence Jewry C; St Lawrence Pountney C; St Leonard Eastcheap A; St Leonard Foster W & C; St Leonard Shoreditch L15; Limehouse C1; Littleton M19; St Luke Old Street P14; St Magnus the Martyr L; St Margaret New Fish Street C; St Margaret Lothbury L; St Margaret Moses L; St Margaret Pattens C; St Margaret Westminster M & W 18; St Martin in the Fields W & L; Precincts of St Martin-le-Grand W; St Martin Ironmonger Lane C; St Martin Ludgate L; St Martin Orgar C; St Martin Outwich C; St Martin Vintry C; St Mary Abchurch L; St Mary Aldermanbury C; St Mary Aldermary A; St Mary-le-bone C1; St Mary Bothaw A; St Mary le Bow A; St Mary Colechurch L; St Mary at Hill L; St Mary Magdalene Old Fish Street L; St Mary Magdalene Milk Street C; St Mary Mounthaw L; St Mary Somerset L; St Mary Staining L; St Mary le Strand M; St Mary Woolchurch Haw C; St Mary Woolnoth L; St Matthew Friday Street C; St Michael Bassishaw L; St Michael Cornhill C; St Michael Crooked Lane A; St Michael Queenhithe L; St Michael le Quern L; St Michael Royal A; St Michael Wood Street C; St Michael Bread Street C; St Mildred Poultry C; South Mimms C1; St Nicholas Acons C; St Nicholas Cole Abbey C; St Nicholas Olave C; Northolt C3; Norwood D10; St Olave Hart Street L; St Olave Old Jewry C; St Olave Silver Street L; St Olave Southwark S; Paddington M & W11; St Pancras (Middx) P6; St Pancras Soper Lane A; St Paul Covent Garden M; St Peter Cornhill L; St Peter near Paul's Wharf C; St Peter le Poer C; St Peter ad Vincula, Tower*; St Peter Westcheap L; Pinner D4; Poplar C1; Precinct of Portpool P; Ruislip C3; St Saviour Southwark S; St Sepulchre C; Shadwell St Paul C; Shepperton M19; Shoreditch P; Staines M19; Stanmore C1; Stanwell M19; St Stephen Coleman Street C; St Stephen Walbrook L; Stepney C; Stoke Newington P7; Sunbury M19; St Swithin London Stone C; Teddington C20; St Thomas the Apostle L; Tottenham C1; Trinity the Less L; Trinity in the Minories L; Twickenham M19; Uxbridge M19; St Vedast Foster Lane A; Wapping St John C; Precincts of Westminster Abbey W; Whitechapel C1; Willesden P5.

* It is not clear into which court's jurisdiction St Peter ad Vincula fell.

Monmouthshire

See with **South Wales**, pages 56-57.

Norfolk

Since 1858: Probate records for England and Wales are at the Principal Registry of the Family Division, Somerset House, Strand, London WC2R 1LP. Indexes to these are held locally at the Norwich Probate Sub-Registry, 65 Cathedral Close, Norwich NR1 4DN (tel. 0603 26648); for other copies, see page 1.

Registered copy wills proved at Norwich, 1858-1941, are deposited at the Norfolk Record Office and are indexed.

Pre-1858: Norfolk was in the province of Canterbury and diocese of Norwich. Apart from P.C.C. (see page 2) virtually all probate records for the county are at the

Norfolk Record Office, Norwich
(0603 611277 ext 262)

The Norfolk probate records comprise:
(1) **Consistory Court of Norwich** (jurisdiction throughout the county and diocese including Suffolk and part of Cambridgeshire). Printed indexes to wills, 1370-1603 (Norfolk Record Soc. 16, 21; BRS 69, 73), 1604-1857 (Norfolk R.S. 28,34, 38,47). Admons 1555-1646 (TS calendar), 1666-1857 (MS calendar).
(2) **Archdeaconry of Norfolk** (jurisdiction: southern Norfolk, and parts of north-eastern and north-western Norfolk, see map and list on right). Printed indexes 1453-1603 (Norfolk and Norwich Genealogical Soc., 3, 5 and 10; further vols. in preparation); MS calendars, wills 1604-1857; admons 1541-1618, 1672-1676, 1678-1682, 1687-1857. TS calendar to invs 1728-1774. Unindexed admons, 1670-1671, 1677, 1683-1685.
(3) **Archdeaconry of Norwich** (jurisdiction: most of northern Norfolk, and deaneries of Breccles and Thetford in southern Norfolk; see map and list on right).
Calendars: wills, 1469-1603 (by year), 1604-1652 (TS index), 1660-1857 (by year); admons 1624-1626, 1632-1637, 1660-1688, 1700-1857; invs 1674-1825 (TS). Unindexed admons 1590-1609.
(4) **Peculiar of Castle Rising**, 1624-1723/4. Index "Norfolk Genealogy" 16.
(5) **Peculiar of Great Cressingham**, 1675-1754. Index, "Norfolk Gen.", 16.

Norfolk, continued

(6) **Peculiar of the Dean and Chapter of Norwich** (see map and list for jurisdiction). Wills 1416-1559, 1572, 1585-1857; admons 1448-1548, 1613-1680, 1737-1857. Index "Norfolk Genealogy" 16 (1984), in two sections, 1416-1600, 1600-1857. Invs 1681-1782, index NG.16, pp.53-56.

Parishes in the detached deaneries of Heacham and Burnham (**H**), and Repps and Waxham (**R**), in the archdeaconry of Norfolk; and in the detached deaneries of Breccles (**B**) and Thetford (**T**) in the archdeaconry of Norwich; parishes in the peculiars of the Dean and Chapter of Norwich (**DC**), Castle Rising (**CR**), and Great Cressingham (**GC**); and the parish of Emneth in the diocese of Ely (**E**).

Aldborough R; Antingham R; Arminghall DC7; Ashill B; Ashmanhaugh R; Aylmerton R; Bacton R; Bagthorpe H; Barmer H; Barningham Norwood R; Barningham Town R; East, North and West Barsham, H; Barton Turf R; Barwick H; West Beckham DC1; Beeston Regis and St Lawrence R; Bessingham R; Gt and Newton Bircham H; Bircham Tofts H; Bradfield R; Brancaster H; Breckles B; Brumstead R; Burnham Deepdale, Norton, Overy, Thorpe, Ulpe and Westgate, H; Carbrooke B; Castle Rising CR4; Caston B; Catfield R; Catton DC6; North and South Creake H; Gt Cressingham GC8; Cromer R; Crostwight R; Dilham R; Docking H; Dunton H; Eaton DC7; Eccles R; Edingthorpe R; Little Ellingham B; Emneth E9; Fakenham H; Felbrigg R; Felmingham R; Fring H; Fulmodeston cum Croxton H; Gatesend H; Gimingham R; Gresham R; Griston R; Gunton R; Hanworth R; Happisburgh R; Heacham H; Hempstead R; Hickling R; Hindolveston DC3; Holme next the Sea H; Honing R; Horning R; Horsey R; Houghton (next Harpley) H; Hoveton St John and St Peter R; Hunstanton H; Ingham R; Ingoldisthorpe H; Irstead R; Kettlestone H; Knapton R; Lakenham DC7; Lessingham R; Ludham R; Martham DC5; Matlask R; Merton B; Metton R; Mundesley R; Neatishead R; Northrepps R; Norwich (Cathedral, St Helen, St James, St Paul) DC7; Overstrand R; Ovington B; Palling R; Paston R; Plumstead DC6; Potter Heigham R; Ridlington R; Ringstead H; Roughton R; Roydon near Lynn CR4; East and West Rudham H; Runton R; East Ruston R; Little Ryburgh H; Saham Toney B; Sco Ruston R; Scoulton B; Sculthorpe H; Sedgeford DC2; Sheringham R; Shernborne H; Sidestrand R; Sloley R; Smallburgh R; Snettisham H; Little Snoring H; Southrepps R; Sprowston DC6; Stalham R; Stanhoe H; Stibbard H; Stow Bedon B; Suffield R; Sustead R; Sutton R; Swafield R; Syderstone H; Tatterford H; Tattersett H; Thetford T; Thompson B; Thornham H; Thorpe Market R; Threxton B; Thurgarton R; Titchwell H; Tottington B; Trimingham R; Trowse Newton DC7; Trunch R; Tunstead R; Walcott R; North Walsham R; Waterden H; Watton B; Waxham R; Westwick R; Witton (near North Walsham) R; North and South Wootton CR4; Worstead R.

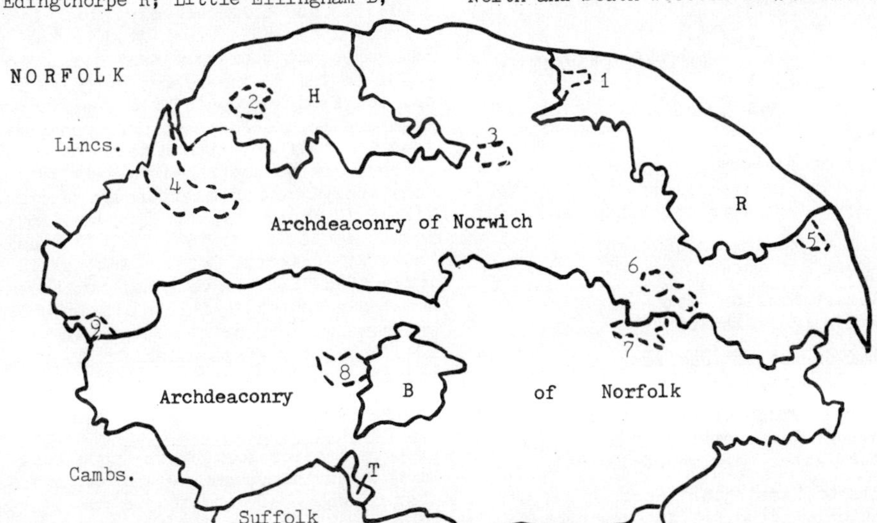

Northamptonshire and Rutland

(Soke of Peterborough now in Cambs.; Rutland now in Leicestershire)

Since 1858: Probate records for England and Wales are at the Principal Registry of the Family Division, Somerset House, Strand, London WC2R 1LP. Indexes to these to 1928 or later are held locally at the Birmingham Reference Library; County Record Office, Huntingdon; Leicestershire Record Office; and the Bodleian Library, Oxford; for other copies, see page 1.

Wills proved at Northampton, 1858-1930 (card index to 1880; in annual volumes 1881-1908) and Peterborough, 1858-1941 (indexed) are held locally at Northants Record Office. Original wills proved at Northampton, 1858-1930, are at Birmingham District Probate Reg., Cavendish House, Waterloo St., Birmingham B2 5PS.

Peculiar of Banbury (Oxon), 7
Kings Sutton (Northants);
Grimsbury (Northants)(parish of Banbury)

Peculiar of Empingham (Rutland), 1
Empingham, Hardwick

Peculiar of Gretton (Northants)
Duddington (3), Gretton (5)

Peculiar of Ketton (Rutland), 2
Ketton, Geeston, Tixover

Peculiar of Liddington (Rutland), 4
Liddington; Caldecott;
Thorpe by Water (parish of Seaton)

Peculiar of Nassington (Northants), 6
Nassington, Apethorpe, Woodnewton, Yarwell.

Before 1858: Northamptonshire and Rutland were in the province of Canterbury and diocese of Peterborough.

Apart from P.C.C. (see page 2), probate records for virtually the whole of both counties are at the

Northamptonshire Record Office,
Northampton (0604 62129)

which issues a leaflet listing the various series of probate records there.

Since the 1590s the major, southern, part of Northamptonshire has been in the jurisdiction of the **Archdeaconry Court of Northampton**; the remainder of the county, the Soke of Peterborough and Rutland, were in the jurisdiction of the **Consistory Court of Peterborough.**

Before 1598 both courts had concurrent jurisdiction, so records from places in either area may be found in either court; but the bulk were always in the Northampton Archdeaconry Court. Records of both courts are at the Northants R.O.

There is a published index to wills in the **Northampton Archdeaconry Court**, 1510-1652, BRS 1; and MS indexes by H.I. Longden 1652-75, 1676-1704, 1704-1751, 1752-1857. These are being superseded by a card index, 1726-1826, and in progress.

Calendars (with indexes) have been published to admons, 1545-46, 1638-41, 1660-1676 (by H.I. Longden); 1677-1800 (BRS 70, 92; Banbury Hist Soc 17). MS calendars, by year, by H.I. Longden, 1801-1820 and orig calendars, 1821-1857.

Invs, 1660-1800, are listed in the BRS vols, but there are many more, 1660-1670, in the MS calendars, which were omitted from Longden's published volume. Visitors to the Northants R.O. should consult staff on which indexes to use.

There are no published indexes to the **Consistory Court of Peterborough** records. Wills: MS index (by H.I. Longden) 1541-1646 (gaps 1576-84, 1592-97), TS index 1604-1719 (also at SofG). Admons: TS index 1598-1684 (in original act books). Act books 1682-1819 relate both to wills and admons, with original indexes to 1742 only. Original calendars to wills and admons, 1719-1857.

Exceptions:

Lincolnshire Archives Office holds probate records for several peculiars in both Northamptonshire and Rutland, most of which are indexed in BRS 57. There are microfilms of the documents at the Northants R.O.

Northamptonshire and Rutland continued

The Peculiars were, in Northamptonshire: **Gretton** with **Duddington** 1657-1832 (BRS 57); **Nassington** 1654-1753 (BRS 57), 1746-1844 (MS list); in Rutland: **Empingham** 1669-1744 (BRS 57), 1745-1835 (MS list); **Ketton** with **Liddington** 1666-1677 (BRS 57)(and see below).

Places in peculiars also occur in the records of the **Peculiar of the Dean and Chapter of Lincoln**, 1534-1834 (BRS 57).

Records of the Rutland peculiars of **Caldecott**, 1669-1820, and **Ketton and Liddington**, 1722-1820, are at the Leicestershire Record Office, printed index in BRS 51; and a few later records on card index.

The Northamptonshire parish of Kings Sutton, and Grimsbury, in the parish of Banbury, were in the **Peculiar of Banbury** with records at the Oxfordshire Record Office, fully indexed, 1547-1856, in Oxon Record Soc 40 and Banbury Hist Soc 1; Grimsbury will and inv abstracts 1591-1650 in Banbury Hist Soc 13, 14.

Northumberland

(Newcastle upon Tyne now in Tyne and Wear)

Since 1858: Probate records for England and Wales are at the Principal Registry of the Family Division, Somerset House, Strand, London WC2R 1LP. Indexes to these are held locally at the Newcastle District Probate Registry, Plummer House, Croft St., Newcastle upon Tyne NE1 6NP.

Registered copy wills proved at Newcastle, 1858-1941 (from 1926 also incl. Gateshead and places immediately south of the River Tyne) are deposited at the Northumberland Record Office.

Before 1858: see with **Durham**, page 15.

Nottinghamshire

Since 1858: Probate records for England and Wales are at the Principal Registry of the Family Division, Somerset House, Strand, London WC2R 1LP. Indexes to these (to 1928) are held locally at the Nottinghamshire Record Office. For other copies, see page 1.

Registered copy wills to 1939 proved at Nottingham (to 1926 for Notts only), indexed to 1935, are held locally at the Nottinghamshire Record Office.

Before 1858: Nottinghamshire was in the province and diocese of York. The county lay entirely (peculiars excepted) in the archdeaconry of Nottingham.

The original records of the archdeaconry and of the peculiars are now at

Nottinghamshire Record Office,
Nottingham (0602 504524)

which has a brief guide for genealogists in preparation. There is a recently completed card index to all probate records for the **Archdeaconry of Nottingham** for the whole period from c.1500-1857.

There is also a separate card index to all probate records for the various **Peculiars**, including the important **Peculiar of Southwell**, from 1506 for the whole period.

Only the original wills of the archdeaconry are at Nottingham, many of which have not survived. There should usually be a registered copy at the

Borthwick Institute, York
(0904 59861 ext 274)

bound in with all the other exchequer and prerogative copy wills, within the period 1389-1857, whilst those at Nottingham do not represent a complete set.

Nottinghamshire wills are also to be found in the **Prerogative Court of York**, at the Borthwick Institute. There are printed indexes to wills and admons for both **Prerogative** and **Exchequer Courts of York** (which include the Nottingham archdeaconry), indexed jointly, 1389-1688 (Yorks Arch Soc Record Series, 6, 11, 14, 19, 22, 24, 26, 28, 32, 35, 49, 60, 68, 89). There is also a printed index to Notts wills and admons only (extracted from these volumes), 1568-1619.

For 1688-1731 there is a TS index available at the Borthwick Institute (where the records are) and at the Nottinghamshire R.O. There is a MS 19th century calendar to records after 1731, to 1857.

There are also a few records for the **Peculiars of Apesthorpe** or Habblesthorpe (1577-1844) and **Bole** (1546-1847)(TS indexes) at the Borthwick Institute.

Nottinghamshire testators are also to be found in the records of P.C.C. (see page 2), although, being in the province of York, these are far fewer than for counties in the southern province. The Nottinghamshire R.O. has a copy of the printed index to P.C.C., 1853-1857.

For a map and list, see page 32.

Nottinghamshire, continued

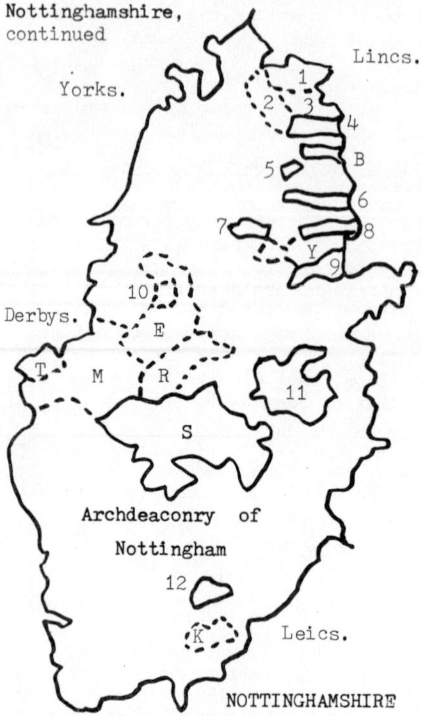

Places in Nottinghamshire in jurisdictions other than the archdeaconry of Nottingham, though they are nevertheless also likely to be found in the exchequer (archdeaconry) records too.

A : Prebend of Apesthorpe; **B** : Prebend of Bole; **E** : Manor of Edwinstowe; **G** : Manor of Gringley-on-the-Hill; **J** : Manor of St John of Jerusalem or Shelford St Johns; **K** : Peculiar of Kinoulton; **M** : Manor of Mansfield; **R** : Manor of Rufford Abbey; **S** : Peculiar of Southwell; **T** : Manor of Skegby and Teversal; **Y** : Peculiar of the Dean and Chapter of York.

Note. The manorial court of St John of Jerusalem (J) had jurisdiction, over tenants of the manor only, in a number of places in the south of the county - these are not marked on the map.

Apesthorpe A6; Askham Y; Aslockton J; Barnby-in-the-Willows J; Beckingham S&G 4; Bleasby S; Blidworth S; Bole B; Budby M10; Calverton S; Carburton E; Car Colston J; Carlton in Gedling J; Carlton on Trent S11; Caunton S11; Cotgrave J; Cropwell Bishop S12; Darlton S9; East Drayton Y; Dunham S9; Eaton S7; Edingley S; Edwinstowe E; Farnsfield S; Flintham J; Gedling J; Gringley-on-the-Hill G2; Halam S; Halloughton S; Hickling J; Holme S11; Hoveringham J; Hucknall under Huthwaite M; Kilton (Worksop) M; Kinoulton K; Kirklington S; Kneeton J; Laneham Y; North Leverton S6; Mansfield M; Mansfield Woodhouse M; Misterton G & Y1; Morton S; North and South Muskham S11; Normanton-on-Soar J; Normanton-on-the-Wolds J; Norwell S11; Owthorpe J; Oxton S; Plumtree J; Radcliffe-on-Trent J; Ragnall S9; Rampton S8; Rempstone J; Ruddington J; Rufford R; Scarrington J; Scofton (Worksop) M; Skegby T; Southwell S; Stanford-on-Soar J; West Stockwith G&Y1; Stokeham Y; Sutton-in-Ashfield M; Teversal T; Tollerton J; Upton S; Walkeringham G3; Warsop M; South Wheatley S5; Willoughby-on-the-Wolds J; Woodborough S; Worksop M.

Oxfordshire

Since 1858: Probate records for England and Wales are at the Principal Registry of the Family Division, Somerset House, Strand, London WC2R 1LP. Indexes to these (to 1928) are held locally at the Bodleian Library, Oxford (Radcliffe Camera, Lower Reading Room, on open shelves). There is a charge of £1 per (2-day) visit. For other copies, see page 1.

Before 1858: Oxfordshire was in the province of Canterbury and formed the diocese and archdeaconry of Oxford.

Apart from P.C.C. (see page 1, and right), probate records for virtually the whole county are held at the

Oxfordshire Record Office, County Hall, New Road, Oxford OX1 1ND
(0865 815203)(appointment necessary).

Oxfordshire, continued

The probate records at the Oxfordshire Record Office comprise:

1. **Consistory and Archdeaconry Courts of Oxford**, covering the whole county except for peculiars. Consolidated index to all probate records, 1528-1732 (published, BRS 93,94); 1738-1800 card index; 1801-1857 card index in progress. Invs 1550-1590 printed in Oxon Record Soc 44, from Oxford consistory, archdeaconry and peculiar courts.
2. **Oxfordshire Peculiars** - the areas round Banbury in the north and Dorchester and Thame in the south - for which there is a joint MS index, 1542-1857. This includes Newington, in the **Peculiar of Monks Risborough**, whose records, 1605-1856, are now at Bucks R.O., page 7.

There is also a printed index to probate records of the **Peculiar of Banbury and Cropredy**, 1542-1857, and the **Manorial Court of Sibford Gower**, 1733-1829 (Oxon Record Soc 40 and Banbury Hist Soc 1); and abstracts of wills, admons and invs for Banbury itself, 1591-1650, are printed in Banbury H.S. 13 and 14. Mid-16th cent records for the peculiars are also found in the consistory and archdeaconry court records.

3. **Court of the Chancellor of the University of Oxford.** These records are not administered by the Bodleian Library, and application to see them must be made to the Deputy Keeper of the University Archives, c/o Bodleian. Jurisdiction was restricted to resident members of the University, but others having connections with the University may appear in the records. There is a printed index to the complete period, wills and admons 1436-1814, invs 1443-1740 ("An Index to Wills Proved in the Court of the Chancellor", 1862).

Oxfordshire Testators in P.C.C.

Wills, 1393-1510, are printed in full in Oxon Record Soc 39.

Printed indexes: full BRS (and others) series to 1700 on open shelves in Selden End, Dept. of Western MSS. Full index to England and Wales, 1853-1858, on open shelves in Radcliffe Camera, Lower Reading Room; printed indexes to Oxfordshire testators in P.C.C., 1750-1800, A-G only, in Oxon FH **1**, 6, pp.166-168, **3**, 6, pp.192-5 (from pubd. index); and to all Oxon and Berks testators for year 1801, Oxon FH, I, 8, pp.216-20. Invs 1661-early C18, listed by parish in "Oxon Local History" I, 2 & 3 (1981).

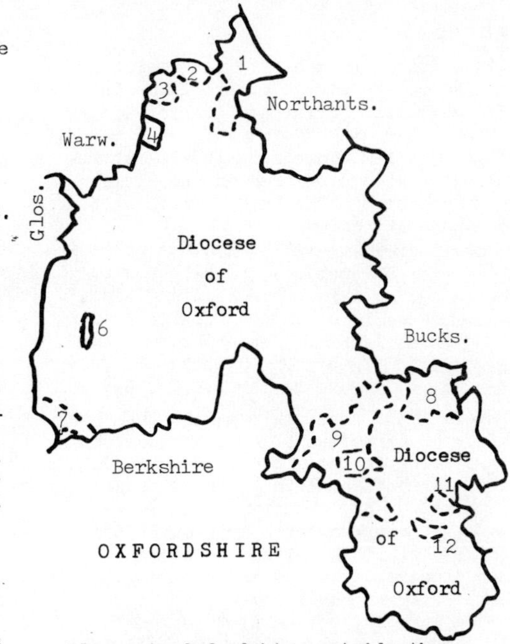

Places in Oxfordshire outside the jurisdiction of the consistory and archdeaconry courts of Oxford:

B : Peculiar of Banbury and Cropredy
M : Peculiar of Monks Risborough

Banbury B1; Benson (Bensington) 9; Britwell Prior 9; Chiselhampton 9; Clifton Hampden 9; Claydon B1; Cropredy B1; Dorchester 9; Drayton St Leonard 9; Horley B2; Hornton B2; Langford 7; Marsh Baldon 9; Gt Milton 9; Mollington B1; Nettlebed 12; Newington M10; Pishill 11; Shenington (Glos., see page 17) 3; Sibford (par of Swalcliffe) 4; Stadhampton 9; Sydenham 8; Tetsworth 8; Thame 8; Toot Baldon 9; Warborough 9; Wardington B1; Widford (Glos.) 6.

Rutland

(now in Leicestershire)

Since 1858: Rutland was in the Leicester probate district and (in addition to the Principal Registry, page 1) registered copy wills proved at Leicester, 1858-1940 are deposited at the Leicestershire Record Office (card index in progress). Original wills, 1858-1969, are still at Leicester Probate Registry (page 24).

Before 1858: see with **Northamptonshire**, pages 30-31.

Shropshire

Since 1858: Probate records for England and Wales are at the Principal Registry of the Family Division, Somerset House, Strand, London WC2R 1LP. Indexes to these (to 1928) are held locally at the Cheshire Record Office and the Birmingham Reference Library; for other copies, see page 1.

Registered copy wills proved at Shrewsbury (for Shropshire), 1858-1940, are deposited at Shropshire Record Office, card indexed 1858-c.1920. Original wills 1930-42 are at the Chester Probate Sub-Registry, 17 Cuppin St., Chester CH1 2DA; earlier wills are at the P.R.O., Hayes.

Before 1858: Shropshire was in the province of Canterbury, the south-western half lying in the diocese of Hereford and the north-eastern in the diocese of Lichfield (and Coventry); with a few extreme north-western parishes in the diocese of St Asaph; and Halesowen in the diocese of Worcester. There were also several peculiars.

The location of the probate records in diocesan record offices reflect this division, most being at Lichfield or Hereford, and some at the National Library of Wales, Aberystwyth. For P.C.C. see page 2.

Places in Shropshire outside the jurisdictions of the consistory courts of Lichfield and Hereford.

Diocese of St Asaph
Kinnerley, Knockin, Llanyblodwel, Llanmynech, Melverley, Oswestry, St Martins, Selattyn, Whittington.

Royal Free Chapel of Shrewsbury St Mary
Albrighton (5); Astley (6); Clive (4); Shrewsbury St Mary (7)

Peculiar of Longdon on Tern (8)

Peculiar of Wombridge Abbey (9)

Peculiar of Ashford Carbonell (12)

Peculiar Deanery of Bridgnorth
Bridgnorth (10); Alveley (11); Bobbington (11); Claverley (11); Quatford (10).

Manor of Ellesmere (1)
Ellesmere, Colemeare, Lyneal, Welshampton

Peculiar of Prees
Calverhall (3); Darliston (3); Prees (3); Whixall (2)

Diocese of Worcester
Halesowen (Salop, detached)

<u>Lichfield Joint Record Office, Lichfield Library</u>, Bird St., Lichfield (05432 56787)

Consistory Court of Lichfield, wills and admons, 1516-1857, 19th century MS calendar; a less accurate version of this to 1652 is printed in BRS 7.

Peculiar of Prees or Pipe Major
Wills 1697-1857, included in consolidated 19th century MS calendar to most peculiars at Lichfield, and printed to 1652 in BRS 7.

Records of other Shropshire peculiars (recently transferred from the National Library of Wales) are

Bridgnorth, 1635-1857 (printed index, Salop Archaeological & Natural History Soc. Transactions, 4th series, vol.12, pt.1, 1929).

Ellesmere, C17-1857 (index SANHS Trs. vol.12, pt.2 (XLV), 1930).

Tyrley, Buildwas, Longdon-on-Tern, Wombridge, Shrewsbury St Mary, C17-1857 (index, SANHS, vol.46, pt.1, 1931).

<u>Record Office, Harold St., Hereford</u> (0432 265441)

Episcopal Consistory Court of Hereford (recently transferred from the National Library of Wales). Card index to wills 1600-1660. Chronological list, wills and invs, 1539-1599, invs 1628-1641. After 1660, to 1857, indexes in act books to wills and admons.

Peculiar of Ashford Carbonell
Wills, admons, invs 1662-1857 (act book).

SHROPSHIRE

Shropshire, continued

A consolidated index to all records in the Hereford consistory courts and peculiars is in preparation for publication by the BRS.

Records of nine parishes in north-western Shropshire in the diocese of **St Asaph** are at the National Library of Wales, Aberystwyth, see page 55.

Shropshire County Library, Shrewsbury, has wills and invs, 1665-1816 for the **Manor of Ruyton-of-the-Eleven-Towns.** Printed index to wills 1665-1709 (64 only) in "Salop.Arch.Soc.Trans.", vcl. 52, pp.116-18. Remainder unindexed.

See also "A List of Wills and Marriage Settlements in the Local History Collection of the Shrewsbury Public Library", 1958 (mainly probate copies).

Halesowen, formerly a detached part of Shropshire, was in the jurisdiction of the **Consistory Court of Worcester,** at Worcester Record Office, printed indexes to 1652 (BRS 31,39), TS index 1660-1857.

Prerogative Court of Canterbury (see also page 2). Printed index to Shropshire wills 1700-1749 in "Shropshire Probates" by G.F. Matthews, 1929; and 1750-1770, MS at S of G.

Somerset

(the northern part of the county is now in the county of Avon)

Since 1858: Probate records for England and Wales are at the Principal Registry of the Family Division, Somerset House, Strand, London WC2R 1LP. Indexes to these are held locally at the Bristol Record Office (1858-1900) and at Exeter (at present at Exeter Probate Sub-Registry, 94 Fore St., Exeter EX4 3HZ, tel 0392 74515; but those over 50 years old may be transferred to Devon County Library); for other copies, see page 1.

Before 1858: Somerset was in the province of Canterbury and diocese of Bath and Wells.

For records of P.C.C., see page 2; also printed abstracts of Somerset wills in P.C.C., 1383-1558 (Somerset Record Soc., vols. 16, 19, 21).

All probate records for the diocese of Bath and Wells deposited in the probate registry at Exeter were destroyed by enemy action in 1942, so there are virtually no original records for the county apart from those in P.C.C.

There are printed indexes to the lost wills and admons for the **Archdeaconry of Taunton**, 1537-1799 (BRS 45, 53) and **Peculiar of Ilminster**, 1690-1857 (BRS 53); and to lost wills, 1528-1600, in Somerset R.S., vol.62, to the following jurisdictions:

Episcopal Consistory Court of Bath and Wells; Consistory Court of the Archdeaconry of Wells; Consistory Court of the Dean of Wells; and **Consistory Court of the Dean and Chapter of Wells.**

There are MS indexes to the destroyed records at SofG, Episcopal Consistory to 1829; Archdeaconry of Wells, to 1799; Dean of Wells, to 1804; Dean and Chapter of Wells, wills to 1720, 1837-1857, admons, 1660-1857; Peculiars (by individual peculiar) c.1660-1857.

The Somerset Record Office, Taunton (0823 87600/78805)

has **Estate Duty Office** copies of most wills for the county from 1812 (for local courts and P.C.C.), card indexed. Also a MS collection of 32 vols. by F.A. Crisp, of P.C.C. and local court abstracts (partially printed in 6 vols., "Abstracts of Somerset Wills ..."). Also card index to 'stray' wills in collections deposited at the Som. R.O.

Wills and admons 1805-1811 should be found amongst the **Death Duty Registers** abstracts at the Public Record Office (see page 4).

Exception:

The Somerset parish of Abbots Leigh was in the jurisdiction of the **Consistory Court of Bristol**, records at the Bristol Record Office, page 17.

Other printed sources:

"Somerset Parishes: a handbook of historical reference to all places in the county", A.L. Humphreys, 1905, indexes many wills by parish.

"Wills of Wellington and West Buckland" 1372-1811, A.L. Humphreys, 1908.

"The Municipal Records of Bath", 1189-1604, A.J. King and B.H. Watts, Appx.A, Part II.

Abstracts of wills, 1530-1599 (225) for Chew Magna, Chew Stoke, Dundry and Stowey in Somerset Record Soc., vol.62.

Somerset, continued

Somerset parishes outside archdeaconry jurisdiction:

B: Consistory court of Bristol; **C**: Consistory court of the Dean and Chapter of Wells; **D**: Consistory court of the Dean of Wells; **I**: Royal peculiar court of Ilminster; **P**: other Wells peculiar and prebendal courts.

Abbots Leigh B2; (Chapel) Allerton D10; Ashill P30; South Barrow C27; Biddisham D6; Binegar D8; Bishops Lydeard C20; Broomfield D21; Buckland Dinham P9; Carhampton D13; Cheddar C7; Chesterblade D17; Chilcompton D8; Combe St Nicholas C32; Compton Bishop P5; Compton Dundon P22; Cudworth P33; North Curry C25; St Decumans P14; Dinder D10; Easton in Gordano P1; Evercreech D17; Fitzhead (pec. of Wiveliscombe) P19; East Harptree P4; Haselbury Plucknett P34; West Hatch C25; Henstridge P29; Ilminster I-31; Ilton P30; Kenn (pec. of Yatton) P3; Kingsbury Episcopi P28; Knowle (pec. of Cudworth) P33; East Lambrook (pec. of Kingsbury) P28; Litton P4; Lovington C24; Bishops Lydeard C20; West Lydford P23; Mark D10; Pilton P16; Priddy D10; St Decumans P14; Stoke St Gregory C35; Nether Stowey D15; Long Sutton C26; Timberscombe P12; Wedmore D10; Wells (St Cuthbert) D10; (Liberty of St Andrews) C10; Westbury D10; Whitelackington P30; Winsham C35; Witham Friary P18; Wiveliscombe P19; Wookey P11; North Wootton P16; Yatton P3.

Staffordshire and Derbyshire

(the southern tip of Staffordshire, round Walsall, Wednesbury, West Bromwich and Wolverhampton, is now in the county of West Midlands)

Since 1858: Probate records for England and Wales are at the Principal Registry of the Family Division, Somerset House, Strand, London WC2R 1LP. Indexes to these (to 1928) are held locally at the Birmingham Reference Library and at Nottinghamshire Record Office; for other copies, see page 1.

Registered copy wills proved at Lichfield (for Staffordshire) 1858-1928 are deposited at the Lichfield Joint Record Office (indexed); those proved at Derby (for Derbyshire) 1858-1928 are at the Derbyshire Record Office, Matlock (also indexed). Original wills proved at Lichfield (to 1928) are at the Birmingham District Probate Registry, Cavendish House, Waterloo St., Birmingham B2 5PS.

Before 1858: Staffordshire and Derbyshire were in the diocese of Lichfield and province of Canterbury.

Apart from P.C.C. (see page 2), virtually all the probate records for both counties are at

Lichfield Joint Record Office, Lichfield Library, Bird St., Lichfield WS13 6PN (05432 56787)

Staffordshire and **Derbyshire**, continued

Places in the jurisdiction of courts other than the consistory court of Lichfield. All places in peculiars are likely to appear also in the consistory court records, and some places not actually in peculiars may still nevertheless be found in records of peculiars.

Staffordshire
(places in area 'B' unless otherwise shown, except Stafford St Chad.)
Clent and Dudley were in the diocese of Worcester

Acton Trussell; Adbaston 7; Alrewas; Upper Arley 13; Armitage; Baswich; Bednall; Bentley; Bilbrook; Bilston; Blithbury; Branstone 5; Brewood; Bromley Regis; Broughton 7; Brownhills; Burton on Trent 5; Bushbury; Cannock; Charnes 7; Chorlton 7; Clent 14; Codsall; Colwich; Compton in Tettenhall; Congreve; Coppenhall; Cotes 7; Drayton in Hales 6; Dudley (Worcs) 11; Dunston; Eccleshall 7; Edingale 9; Farewell; Fradley; Fradswell 8; Gnosall 7; Hammerwich; Handsacre; Harborne 12; Haselour; Hatherton; Great Haywood; Hilton in Wolverhampton; Hints; Horninglow 5; Kings Bromley; Kinvaston; Levedale; **Lichfield**; Longdon; Mavesyn Ridware; Norton Canes; Oaken; High Offley 7; Ogley Hay; Packington; Pattingham; Pelsall; Penkridge; Perton; Pipe Ridware; Rodbaston; Rugeley; Saredon; Sedgley 10; Shareshill; Shobnall 5; Shugborough; Slindon 7; Smethwick 12; Stafford St Chad; Streethay; Stretton in Burton 5; Stretton in Penkridge; Sugnall 7; Swinfen; Tettenhall; Tipton; Trescott; Tyrley 6; Wall; Walton 7; Water Eaton; Wednesfield; Weeford; The Wergs; Wetmore 5; Whittington; Willenhall; Wolverhampton; Wrottesley; Wyrley; Yoxall.

Derbyshire
(places in area 'A' unless otherwise shown)

Ashford; Bakewell; Baslow; Beeley; Biggin; Breaston 3; Burbage; Buxton; Chapel-en-le-Frith; Chelmorton; Dale Abbey 2; Long Eaton 3; Fairfield; Hartington; Hope; Kniveton 1; Longstone; Monyash; High Needham; Peak Forest; Risley 3; Sandiacre 3; Sawley 3; Sheldon; Stapenhill 4; Earl Sterndale; Taddington; Tideswell; Wilne 3; Winshall 3; Winster; Wormhill.

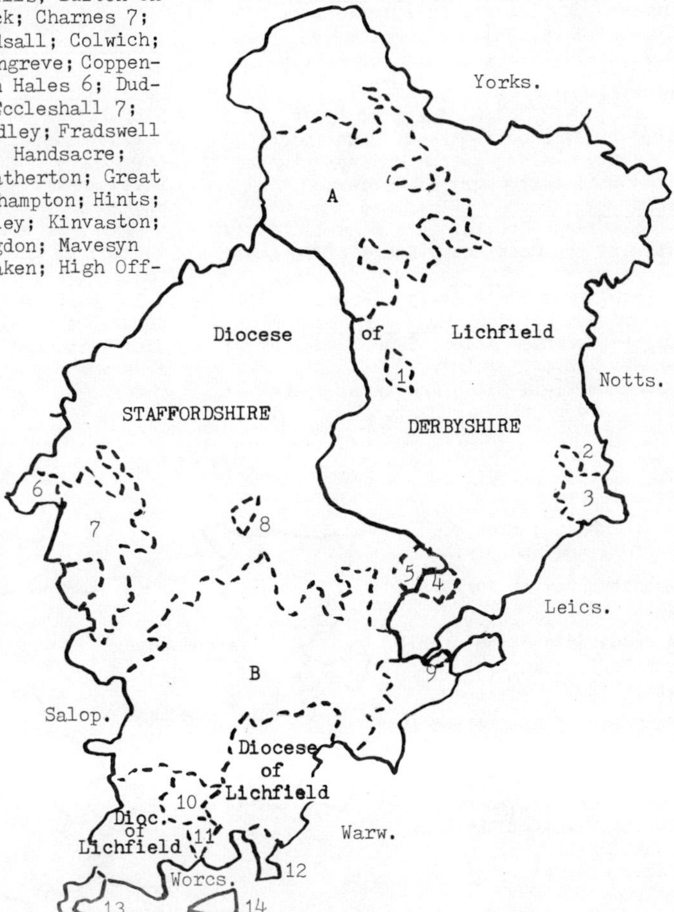

Staffordshire and Derbyshire, continued

The Lichfield Joint Record Office issues a "Handlist to the Diocesan Records" (2nd edn., 1978) summarising the testamentary records.

There are good 19th cent MS calendars to the **Consistory Court of Lichfield**, 1516-1857; and to the various **Peculiars** in the diocese (one consolidated index, 1536-1857). There are less accurate versions of these, to 1652, printed in BRS 7.

Places in peculiars frequently also occur in the consistory court, so that index should always be consulted too.

There is a TS transcript and index of wills and admons in **Colwich Peculiar Court**, 1614-1857, copies at Lichfield J.R.O. and S of G.

The South Yorkshire Record Office has copies of wills and invs for Norton, Dore, Totley, Beighton, Mosbrough, formerly Derbys. but now in South Yorks.

Exceptions:

Drayton-in-Hales, **Manor of Tyrley**, 1695-1841, records now at Lichfield.

Clent, Staffs, in the jurisdiction of the **Consistory Court of Worcester**, Worcester Record Office, see page 45.

Balterley, Staffs, in the jurisdiction of the **Consistory Court of Chester** Cheshire Record Office, see page 9.

Peculiar of Dale Abbey, Derbys, records at Nottinghamshire Record Office, printed index, 1753-1790 (BRS 7) and MS list, 1791-1857.

Chesterfield wills and invs, 1521-1603, are printed in Derbys R.S. vol.1.

Suffolk

Since 1858: Probate records for England and Wales are at the Principal Registry of the Family Division, Somerset House, Strand, London WC2R 1LP. Indexes to these are held locally at the Norwich Probate Sub-Registry, 65 Cathedral Close, Norwich NR1 4DN, tel. 0603 26648; for other copies, see page 1. That formerly at Ipswich has been transferred to the South Yorkshire County Record Office.

Registered copy wills proved at Bury St Edmunds (West Suffolk district) 1858-1928 are now at the Bury St Edmunds branch of the Suffolk Record Office. Those proved at Ipswich (East Suffolk and northern Essex) 1858-1941 are at the Ipswich branch of the Suffolk Record Office, and are indexed.

Before 1858: Suffolk was in the province of Canterbury and diocese of Norwich. The major collections of probate records are at the two branches of the Suffolk Record Office: Ipswich (Archdeaconry of Suffolk, covering East Suffolk); and Bury St Edmunds (Archdeaconry of Sudbury covering West Suffolk). **Suffolk** testators are also to be found in the records of the consistory court of Norwich, at the Norfolk Record Office, as well, of course, as in P.C.C. - see page 2 and page 39, right.

The Suffolk R.O. publishes "A Guide to Genealogical Sources in Suffolk", 2nd edn, 1985, £3 + 70p p&p, which includes a very short section on probate records.

Places in Suffolk outside the jurisdiction of the archdeaconries of Suffolk and Sudbury:

Archdeaconry of Norfolk:
Rushford (2)

Archdeaconry of Norwich:
Thetford, Bramford, Great Finborough (1)

Peculiar of Freckenham
(3)

Peculiar of the Archbishop of Canterbury in the Deanery of Bocking
Monks Eleigh (5)
Hadleigh (6)
Moulton (4)

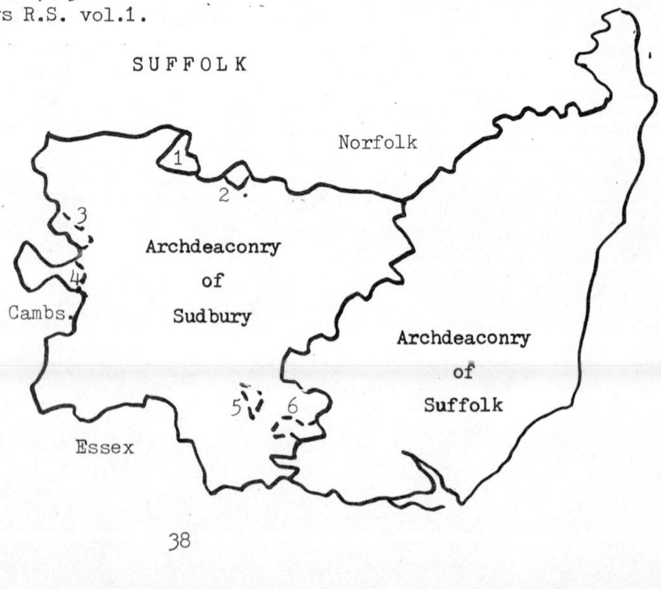

Suffolk, continued

The Ipswich branch of the Suffolk Record Office (0473 55801) has a free leaflet, "Notes for Genealogists at Ipswich". The published index (BRS 90, 91) to all probate records in the **Archdeaconry of Suffolk**, 1444-1702, supersedes Crisp's Calendar, 1444-1600. The card index to later records, 1703-1857, should if possible be used in preference to Gandy's Calendar, 1751-1793 (1929), which has been 'found wanting in many respects'.

Printed abstracts: Ipswich invs 1583-1681 (Suffolk Record Soc 22, 1981).

The Bury St Edmunds branch of the Suffolk Record Office (0284 63141) also issues a free leaflet on "Genealogical Sources". The published index (BRS 95, 96) to all probate records in the **Archdeaconry of Sudbury**, 1354-1700, supersedes that to wills, 1354-1538, in Proc. Suffolk Inst. Arch. 12.
MS index (on m'film), 1701-1799.
Card index, 1800-1857.

Also at this office are the records of the **Peculiar of Isleham** (Cambs) **and Freckenham** (Suffolk). Card index, wills 1556-1856, admons, invs 1661-1817; pre-1701 entries also in BRS 95,96.

Norfolk Record Office, Norwich (0603 611277 ext 262) has records of the **Consistory Court of Norwich.** As this court had superior jurisdiction throughout the diocese, Suffolk testators from throughout the county may be found here. There are printed indexes to wills 1370-1603 (Norfolk Record Soc, 16, 21; BRS 69,73), 1604-1857 (Norfolk R.S. 28,34,38,47). For admons 1555-1857 see page 28.

Exceptions:

Rushford, in the **Archdeaconry of Norfolk**, see page 28.

Thetford, Bramford, Great Finborough, in the **Archdeaconry of Norwich**, page 28.

Monks Eleigh, Hadleigh, Moulton, in the **Peculiar** of the Archbishop of Canterbury in the Deanery of **Bocking**, at Essex Record Office, page 15. Wills 1627-1857 indexed in BRS 79, 84. Also TS abstracts, wills from P.C.C., 1649-1660, admons 1665-83, 1722-38, 1756-1853 (at SofG).

Prerogative Court of Canterbury

There is a printed index to Suffolk wills in P.C.C., 1383-1604 ("Calendar" by T.W. Oswald-Hicks, 1913).

Surrey

Since 1858: Probate records for England and Wales are at the Principal Registry of the Family Division, Somerset House, Strand, London WC2R 1LP; see page 1.

Before 1858: Surrey was in the province of Canterbury and diocese of Winchester apart from the exempt deanery of Croydon, a peculiar of the archbishop of Canterbury.

Apart from P.C.C. (see page 2 and below), most probate records for the county are at the

Greater London Record Office, 40 Northampton Road, EC1R 0AB (01-633 6851).

These comprise:

1. **Commissary Court of the Bishop of Winchester in the Archdeaconry of Surrey.** Wills and admons 1662-1751 (MS calendar); 1752-1857 (index pub by W.Surrey FHS,1983).
2. **Archdeaconry Court of Surrey.** Wills (only) 1480-1751 (MS calendar); 1752-1857 (index pub by W.Surrey FHS, 1981). Abstracts 1480-90,1595-1607 (Surrey RS).

Pre-Commonwealth records of Surrey testators are also to be found at the Hampshire Record Office, Winchester, in the **Consistory Court of Winchester.** TS index of Surrey wills 1606-1645 (copy also at SofG), but note also C16 Surrey wills in main index at Hants R.O.(p.18).

Lambeth Palace Library, London SE1 7JU, has records of the **Peculiar of the Archbishop of Canterbury in the Deanery of Croydon**, including the Surrey parishes of Barnes (2), Burstow (8), Charlwood (7), Cheam (4), Croydon (3), East Horsley (5), Merstham (6), Mortlake (2), Church Newington (1), Putney (2), Roehampton (2), Walworth St Peter (1) and Wimbledon (2).

Good MS index to all records, 1614-1821 (also TS copies at P.R.O. and SofG).

Prerogative Court of Canterbury

Printed abstracts, Surrey wills 1600-1610, Surrey Arch Collns 10-13, 23, 24.

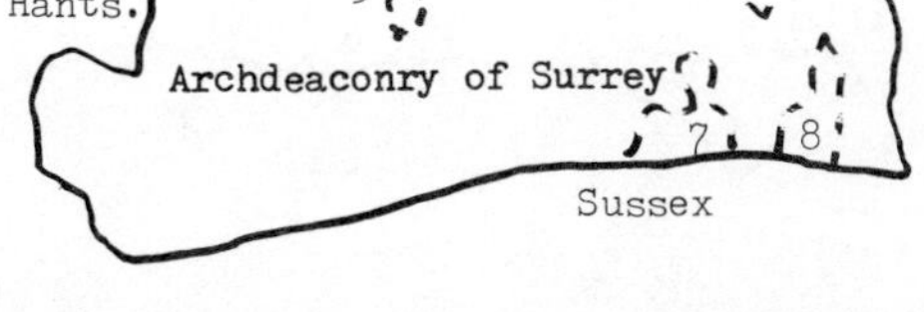

Sussex

See "A Guide to Sussex Probate Records", M.J. Burchall, Sussex Genealogical Centre Occ Ppr 7, 1981, for detailed information.

Since 1858: Probate records for England and Wales are at the Principal Registry of the Family Division, Somerset House, Strand, London WC2R 1LP. Indexes to these (to 1928) are held locally at the East Sussex Record Office, Lewes, and at the Hampshire Record Office, Winchester; for other copies, see page 1.

Registered copy wills proved at Chichester (for West Sussex) to 1928 are deposited at the West Sussex Record Office, Chichester, and are indexed.

Before 1858: Sussex was in the province of Canterbury and diocese of Chichester. The two archdeaconries of Chihcester and Lewes corresponded approximately to the pre-1974 civil divisions of West and East Sussex. Their records are now respectively at the West and East Sussex Record Offices.

West Sussex Record Office, Chichester (0243 777983).

See "Genealogists' Guide to Sources in the W.S.R.O.", P. Wilkinson, 1983.

Apart from P.C.C.(see pages 2 and 41) virtually all probate records for West Sussex are here, the majority in the Consistory Court of the Bishop of Chichester for the **Archdeaconry of Chichester.** There are printed indexes to wills 1479-1800 (BRS 49) and admons 1555-1800 (BRS 64)(see also "Sussex Notes and Queries" 12, pp.37-39 for omitted admons 1675-1676).

Card index, wills and admons 1801-57 and to other wills and admons C16-C18, omitted from printed indexes. Index to invs 1521-1834 pub. on microfiche (1981).

Also at the West Sussex R.O. are the records of the peculiar courts of:
1. **The Dean of Chichester** (jurisdiction over all Chichester parishes except All Saints; also Fishbourne and Rumboldswyke). Printed index, wills 1553-1643, 1660-1800; admons 1577-1626, 1660-1768 (BRS 64); card index to later wills and admons up to 1858 and to others omitted from the printed indexes.
2. **Deaneries of Pagham and Tarring** (for jurisdiction see list and map below). Printed index, wills 1516-1648, admons 1560-1670 (BRS 64); card index to later wills and admons up to 1858 and to others omitted from the printed indexes.

(Pre-1974) West Sussex parishes in the archdeaconry of Lewes:

Beeding, Crawley, Cowfold, Henfield, Kingston, Ifield, Shermanbury, Old and New Shoreham, Southwick, Woodmancote.

Sussex parishes outside the jurisdiction of the archdeaconries of Lewes and Chichester.

B : Deanery of Battle; **C** : Peculiar of the Dean of Chichester; **M** : Deanery of South Malling; **P** : Deaneries of Pagham and Tarring; **R** : Diocese of Rochester.

Battle B5; South Bersted P9; Buxted M3; Chichester All SS P7; Chichester (rest) C7; (The) Cliff M3; Durrington P12; Edburton M13; Fishbourne C7; Framfield M3; Glynde M 3; Heene P12; Isfield M3; Lamberhurst R2; East Lavant P6; St Thomas Lewes M3; Lindfield M4; South Malling M3; Mayfield M3; Pagham P9; Patching P11; Plaistow in Kirdford P1; Ringmer M3; Rumboldswyke C7; Slindon P10; Stanmer M14; Tangmere P8; West Tarring P12; Uckfield M3; Wadhurst M3.

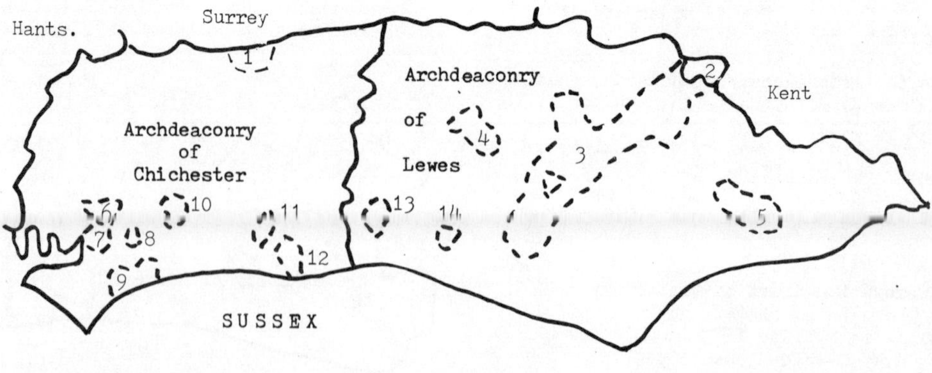

Sussex, continued

Most probate records for East Sussex (apart from P.C.C., see page 2) are at

East Sussex Record Office, Lewes
(0273 475400)

which issues a booklet "How to Trace the History of your Family" summarising the testamentary records in the office; and also a free leaflet "Your County Record Office".

The main holding is that of the Consistory Court of the Bishop of Chichester for the **Archdeaconry of Lewes.** This covers virtually the whole of East Sussex and also the (pre-1974) West Sussex parishes listed on page 40. Printed index to wills and admons 1518-1652 (BRS 24) and TS index 1660-1857.

Also at the East Sussex R.O. are records of two peculiars (for jurisdictions see list and map, page 40):

1. **Deanery of Battle.** Printed indexes, wills 1531-1617, admons 1548, 1572-1617 (BRS 24); wills and admons 1657-1856 ("Sussex Genealogist and Local Histn.", vol.1, no.1, June 1979).
2. **Deanery of South Malling.** Printed indexes: wills and admons 1559-1567 (BRS 64; Sussex Arch Soc Colln, 50, pp.138-146)(these documents are at the West Sussex R.O., but microfilm of them is at the East Sussex R.O.); wills 1588-1646 (BRS 24). Card index (by M.J. Burchall), wills and admons 1559-1857 (see also "Sussex Family Histn.", vol.3 no.2, Sept. 1977).

Exception:

Lamberhurst (Kent and East Sussex) was partly in the jurisdiction of the Consistory and Archdeaconry Courts of Rochester, Kent, see page 22.

Sussex Testators in P.C.C.

There is a printed index to wills of Sussex testators apparently omitted from P.C.C. records, but now at West Sussex R.O. 1614-70 (BRS 64) and TS index.

Warwickshire

(the north-west, Birmingham and Coventry area, is now in West Midlands)

Since 1858: Probate records for England and Wales are at the Principal Registry of the Family Division, Somerset House, Strand, London WC2R 1LP. Indexes to these (to 1928) are held locally at the Birmingham Reference Library, Local Studies Dept.; see also page 1.

Warwickshire, continued

Registered copy wills proved at Birmingham (for Warwickshire) to 1941 are also at the Birmingham Reference Library (not indexed). Original wills are at the Birmingham District Probate Registry, Cavendish House, Waterloo Street, Birmingham B2 5PS, tel. 021-236 6262.

Before 1858: Warwickshire was in the province of Canterbury and split between the dioceses of Lichfield and Worcester. As a result, the main collections of probate records are outside the county (and the modern county of West Midlands). For P.C.C. see page 2.

Records of the major, north-eastern, part of the county are at the

Lichfield Joint Record Office, Lichfield Library, Bird St., Lichfield WS13 6PN
(05432 56787)

which issues a "Handlist to the Diocesan Probate and Church Commissioners' Records" (2nd edn, 1978), summarising the testamentary records.

There is a good 19th century calendar to the **Consistory Court of Lichfield**, wills and admons, 1516-1857. A separate index to records of **Peculiars** there includes the parishes of Arley, Bishops Itchington, Bishops Tachbrook, Edgbaston and Merevale, wills and admons 1536-1857 (one consolidated index). There are less accurate printed versions of these indexes to 1652 in BRS 7.

Records of the south-western part of the county are mainly at the

Record Office, County Hall, Worcester
(Hereford and Worcester C.C.)
(0905 353366 ext 3612)

in the **Consistory Court of Worcester.** The 71 Warwickshire parishes in this diocese are listed on page 42. Printed indexes to wills 1451-1652, admons 1520-1652 (BRS 31,39); TS index to wills, admons and invs, 1660-1857.

The Shakespeare's Birthplace Trust, Stratford upon Avon (0789 204016)

has records of two peculiars (for jurisdictions see list and map, page 42):

1. **Stratford upon Avon**, wills and admons, 1658-1849 (TS index).
2. **Hampton Lucy**, wills, admons and invs 1678-1795 (MS index).

See also the consistory court of Worcester.

County map on page 42.

Warwickshire, continued

Warwickshire Record Office, Warwick (0926 493431 ext 2508)

holds records of the **Peculiars of Baddesley Clinton, Barston, Knowle, Packwood** and **Temple Balsall.** Printed index wills and admons 1675-1790 (BRS 7). MS calendar, post-1790 records; also Temple Balsall 1652-1741, copy at Worcester Record Office.

Exceptions:

Welford and Weston-upon-Avon, in the jurisdiction of the **Consistory Court of Gloucester**, Gloucestershire R.O., p.17.

Mollington (partly Oxon) in parish of Cropredy (Oxon), in the jurisdiction of the **Peculiar of Banbury and Cropredy**, at the Oxfordshire Record Office, see page 33.

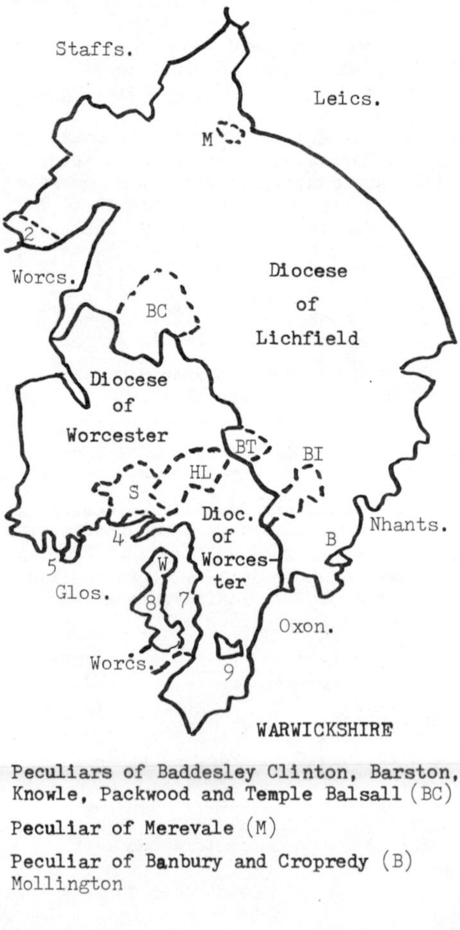

Peculiars of Baddesley Clinton, Barston, Knowle, Packwood and Temple Balsall (BC)

Peculiar of Merevale (M)

Peculiar of Banbury and Cropredy (B)
Mollington

Warwickshire parishes in the **diocese of Worcester:**

Alcester, Gt Alne, Alveston, Arrow, Aston Cantlow, Atherston on Stour, Barcheston, Barford, Barton on the Heath, Bearley, Beaudesert, Bidford, Billesley, Binton, Brailes, Budbrooke, Burmington, Butlers Marston, Charlecote, Cherington, Claverdon, Long Compton, Compton Verney, Compton Wynyates, Coughton, Eatington, Exhall, Halford, Hampton Lucy, Haseley, Haselor, Hatton, Henley in Arden, Honington, Idlicote, Ilmington (detd. W8), Ipsley, Kineton, Kinwarton, Lapworth, Lighthorne, Loxley, Moreton Morrell, Morton Bagot, Newbold Pacey, Norton Lindsey, Oxhill, Pillerton Hersey and Priors, Preston Bagot, Rowington, Salford, Sherbourne, Snitterfield, Spernall, Stratford upon Avon, Stretton on the Fosse (detd.W8), Studley, Tanworth, Temple Grafton, Tysoe, Ullenhall, Warwick, Wasperton, Weethley, Wellesbourne, Whatcote, Whichford, Whitchurch (detd W8), Wixford, Gt Wolford, Wolverton, Wootton Wawen, Wroxhall.

Peculiar of Stratford upon Avon (S)
Stratford upon Avon, Bishopton, Bridgetown, Clopton, Dodwell, Drayton, Luddington, Shottery, Welcombe.

Peculiar of Hampton Lucy (HL)
Hampton Lucy, Alveston, Charlecote, Wasperton.

Places in these two peculiars also occur in the consistory court of Worcester.

Peculiar of Bishops Itchington (BI)
Bishops Itchington, Chadshunt, Gaydon

Peculiar of Bishops Tachbrook (BT)

Peculiar of the Dean and Chapter of Lichfield
Edgbaston (2)

Diocese of Gloucester
(parishes partly in Glos.)
Welford (5), Weston upon Avon (4), Sutton-under-Brailes (9)

Diocese and County of Worcester (7)
(Worcs. parishes detached)
Alderminster, Shipston on Stour, Tidmington, Tredington

Westmorland

See with **Cumberland**, pages 10 and 11

Wiltshire

Since 1858: Probate records for England and Wales are at the Principal Registry of the Family Division, Somerset House, Strand, London WC2R 1LP. Indexes to these are held locally at the Hampshire Record Office, Winchester (to 1928) and at the Bristol Record Office (to 1900). For other copies, see page 1.

Registered copy wills proved at Salisbury, 1858-1928, are at the Wiltshire Record Office and are indexed.

Before 1858: Wiltshire was in the province of Canterbury and diocese of Salisbury.

Apart from P.C.C. (see page 2) virtually all probate records for the county are at the

Wiltshire Record Office, Trowbridge (022-14 3641 ext 3502)

See "Sources for the History of a Wiltshire Family" (1981).

The county is mainly divided between the **Archdeaconries of Salisbury** (Southern Wiltshire) and **Wiltshire** (northern Wiltshire). There are, however, numerous parishes outside the jurisdiction of either archdeaconry. These were in the **Archdeaconry of the Sub-Dean of Salisbury** or in one of the many **peculiars,** and are listed on page 44. See also the **Consistory Court of Salisbury,** which at times had jurisdiction in all parishes in the county, and had sole jurisdiction in the Bishop's peculiars.

There are no published indexes or calendars. Those at the Wiltshire R.O. are 19th century MS calendars, with modern additions, to all probate records, individually to each court, though a comprehensive card index to all courts is in preparation.

Archdeaconry of Salisbury: wills 1528-1857; admons and invs 1540-1857.

Archdeaconry of Wiltshire: wills 1557-1857, admons and invs 1587-1857 (also TS index to 1799, copy at SofG).

Episcopal Consistory Court of Salisbury: wills 1526-1857, admons and invs 1584-1857.

Other courts in Wiltshire, outside the jurisdiction of the archdeaconries of Salisbury and Wiltshire:-

Archdeaconry of the Sub-Dean of Salisbury (jurisdiction: Salisbury except the Close, Milford, Stratford-sub-Castle): wills 1581-1588, wills, admons and invs 1584, 1611-1857 (modern MS calendar).

Peculiars:

Dean of Salisbury (jurisdiction incl. Salisbury Close and 8 parishes in Wilts, 7 Berkshire parishes and 28 Dorset parishes or chapelries; also occasionally other parishes as shown in the list on page 44): wills, admons and invs 1557-1857 (19th century MS calendar). See also **Miscellaneous Wills** below.

Dean and Chapter of Salisbury: 1600-1857.

Precentor of Salisbury: 1614-1857.

Prebend of Calne: 1610-1857

Dean and Canons of Windsor in Wantage: 1669-1840 (see also court of the Dean of Salisbury).

Castle Combe: 1669-1786 (thereafter see archdeaconry of Wiltshire).

Corsham: wills 1462-1857, admons and invs 1720-1857 (19th century MS chronological list); wills 1662-1799, admons and invs 1720-1799 (TS at SofG). See also archdeaconry of Wiltshire.

Savernake Forest: 1617-1829 (jurisdiction: Great and Little Bedwyn, see also Court of Dean of Salisbury and after 1829; Collingbourne Ducis, see also Consistory Court and after 1829).

For the following **prebendal peculiars** see also the court of the **Dean of Salisbury,** and **Miscellaneous Wills** below:

Bishopstone: 1625-1799, 1800-1854.

Chute and Chisenbury: 1608-1799, 1800-1855.

Coombe and Harnham: 1648-1799, 1800-1855.

Durnford: 1634-1799, 1800-1857.

Highworth: 1609, 1623-1799, 1800-1857.

Hurstbourne and Burbage: 1635-1799, 1800-1856.

Netheravon: 1597-1799, 1800-1854.

Trowbridge: see Miscellaneous Wills.

Wilsford and Woodford: 1615-1854.

Miscellaneous Wills: many of these relate to the courts of the Dean and of the Sub-Dean of Salisbury. Index: wills 1540-1809 (TS, superseding printed index of (Wilts) wills 1540-1809 (Wilts Arch and Nat Hist Mag, vol.45, pp.36-67) but now incomplete).

Exceptions:

Kingswood and Marston Meysey were in the jurisdiction of the **Consistory Court of Gloucester,** page 17.

Whitsbury and West Wellow were in the jurisdiction of the **Consistory Court of Winchester,** pages 18-19.

For a map of the county and list of parishes in peculiars, see page 44.

Wiltshire, continued

Parishes in Wiltshire outside the jurisdiction of the archdeaconries of Salisbury and Wiltshire.

B : Prebend of Bishopstone; **C** : Prebend of Chute and Chisenbury; **CB** : Prebend of Combe (Bissett) and Harnham; **CC** : Peculiar of Castle Combe; **CG** : Consistory Court of Gloucester; **CS** : Consistory Court of Salisbury (in Bishop's Peculiars); **CW** : Consistory and Archdeaconry Courts of Winchester; **D** : Prebend of Durnford; **DC** : Peculiar Court of the Dean of and Chapter of Salisbury; **DS** : Peculiar Court of the Dean of Salisbury; **H** : Prebend of Highworth; **HB** : Prebend of Hurstbourne and Burbage; **N** : Prebend of Netheravon; **P** : Peculiar Court of the Precentor of Salisbury; **SD** : Archdeaconry of the Sub-Dean of Salisbury; **SF** : Peculiar of the Lord Warden of Savernake Forest; **T** : Peculiar of Trowbridge; **TC** : Peculiar Court of the Treasurer in the Prebend of Calne; **VC** : Peculiar of the Perpetual Vicar of Corsham; **W** : Peculiar of the Dean and Canons of Windsor in Wantage; **WW** : Prebend of Wilsford and Woodford.

Alderbury TC38; Baydon DS6; Gt and Lit Bedwyn SF&DS15; Berwick Bassett TC9; Berwick St James CS28; Bishops Cannings DC13; Bishopstone B&DS4; Blackland (Calne) TC8; Bramshaw DC42; Bratton (Westbury) P20; Britford DC37; Broad Blunsdon H&DS2; South Broom DC13; Burbage HB&DS14; Calne TC8; Castle Combe CC5; Cherhill (Calne) TC8; Chisenbury C&DS24; Chute C&DS23; Collingbourne Ducis SF&CS22; Coombe Bissett CB&DS39; Corsham VC&CS7 (also archd. of Wilts); Devizes CS18; Dilton (Westbury) P20; Durnford D&DS30; Farley TC34; Figheldean TC25; (West) Harnham CB&DS35; Heytesbury DS26; Highworth H&DS2; Hill Deverill DS27; Homington DC40; Horningsham DS27; Hungerford W&DS12; Kingswood CG (detd.); Knook DS26; Lake (Wilsford) WW&DS19; West Lavington CS21; Marlborough CS11; Marston Meysey CG1; South Marston H&DS2; Mere DS32; Milford SD&CS33; Netheravon N&DS24; Ogbourne St Andrew and St George W&DS10; Pitton TC34; Potterne CS18; Preshute CS11; Ramsbury DS6; **Salisbury** SD&CS33; Salisbury Close DS33; Sevenhampton H&DS2; Shalbourne W&DS16; Southbroom DC13; Staverton (Trowbridge) CS&T17; Stert CS18; Stratford-sub-Castle SD&CS33; Stratton St Margaret VC&CS3 (also arch of Wilts); Swallowcliffe DS36; Trowbridge CS&T17; Tytherington (Heytesbury) DS26; West Wellow CW42; Westbury P20; Whitsbury or Whichbury CW41; Wilsford WW&DS19; Winterbourne Dauntsey C&DS31; Woodford WW&DS29.

Worcestershire

(now part of Hereford and Worcester; northern tip in West Midlands county)

Since 1858: Probate records for England and Wales are at the Principal Registry of the Family Division, Somerset House, Strand, London WC2R 1LP. Indexes to these are held locally at the Birmingham Reference Library; see also page 1.

Registered copy wills proved at Worcester (for Worcestershire) 1858-1928 are deposited at the Record Office, Worcester. There is a duplicated TS index to these wills, copies at SofG and elsewhere. The original wills 1858-1928 are at the Birmingham Probate Registry, Cavendish House, Waterloo St., Birmingham B2 5PS, tel. 021-236 6262/4560.

Worcestershire, continued

Before 1858: Worcestershire was in the province of Canterbury and diocese of Worcester, apart from a few parishes in the dioceses of Hereford and at times in Gloucester.

Apart from P.C.C. (see page 2) most probate records for the county are at

the Record Office (Hereford and Worcester C.C.), County Hall, Spetchley Road, Worcester WR1 2HN (0905 353366 ext 3612)

The office issues a leaflet on probate records in its custody. These comprise

1. **Consistory Court of Worcester.** By far the most important collection, covering the whole county (and diocese) apart from places listed right.
   Printed indexes, wills 1451-1495, 1509-1652, admons and invs 1520-1652 (BRS 31, 39). TS indexes, 1660-1857 (in four parts).

2. **Dean and Chapter of Worcester,** with jurisdiction over the following peculiars:
   Berrow, 1670-1786;
   Kempsey, 1668-1779;
   Norton nr Kempsey, 1668-1785;
   Stoulton, 1668-1787;
   Tibberton, 1770-1788;
   St Michael in Bedwardine and the College precincts, 1669-1783.
   See also the Consistory Court.

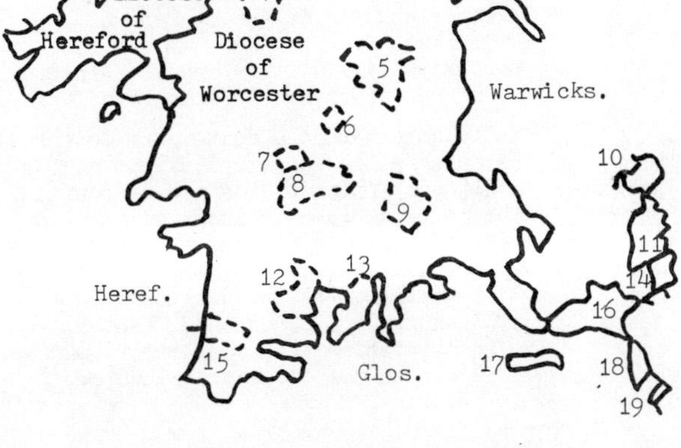

3. **Other peculiars:**
   Alvechurch or Allchurch, 1718-1773;
   Bredon with Norton and Cutsdean, 1718-1773;
   Fladbury (incl. Wyre Piddle, Throckmorton, Stock, Bradbury), 1642-1795;
   Hanbury, 1720-1784 (and act book 1647-1762);
   Hartlebury, 1720-1784;
   Ripple with Queenhill and Holdfast, 1663-1727 (act book), 1721-1779;
   Tredington, 1691-1697 (act book), 1717-1788.

Records of twenty Worcestershire parishes or chapelries (listed below) are at the
Record Office, Hereford
in the jurisdiction of the **Episcopal Consistory Court of Hereford.** Card index to wills, 1600-1660. Chronological list, wills and invs, 1539-1599, invs 1628-1641. Indexes in act books to wills and admons, 1660-1857.

Worcestershire parishes, detached from the main county, or in peculiars, but still also in the jurisdiction of the **Consistory Court of Worcester**; and those in the jurisdiction of the Consistory Court of Hereford.

Detached parishes in the diocese of Worcester:
Alderminster 10; Blockley 16; Daylesford 19; Dudley 1; Evenlode 18; Shipston on Stour 14; Tidmington 14.

Peculiars (also subject to the Consistory Court of Worcester): Alvechurch 3; Berrow 15; Bradbury 9; Bredon 13; Bredons Norton 13; Cutsdean 17; Fladbury 9; Hanbury 5; Hartlebury 4; Holdfast 12; Kempsey 8; Norton (nr Bredon) 13; Norton (nr Kempsey) 8; Queenhill 12; Ripple 12; Stock 9; Stoulton 8; Throckmorton 9; Tibberton 6; Tredington 11; Wolverley 2; Worcester, College Precincts and St Michael in Bedwardine 7; Wyre Piddle 9.

Parishes and chapelries in the diocese of Hereford:
Abberley, Bayton, Bockleton, Clifton on Teme, Eastham, Edvin Loach, Hanley Child and William, Knighton-on-Teme, Kyre Magna and Parva, Lindridge, Mamble, Orleton, Pensax, Rock, Lower Sapey, Stanford-on-Teme, Stockton-on-Teme, Tenbury.

The Province of York

Before 1858: The **Prerogative Court of York** (P.C.Y.) had jurisdiction over the whole province: that is, in addition to the diocese of York itself, the dioceses of Carlisle, Chester, Durham, and Sodor and Man. This jurisdiction was over any person having goods either in more than one jurisdiction within the diocese of York, or in more than one diocese in the northern province, or in both northern and southern provinces. Unless a person is known to have had widespread property it is best to search first the probate records of the diocese in which the deceased died.

At times, two other courts exercised the functions of P.C.Y. These were the **Chancery Court of the Archbishop of York** and the **Court of the Dean and Chapter of York.**

Records of these courts are all at

The Borthwick Institute of Historical Research, St Anthony's Hall, Peasholme Green, York YO1 2PW (0904 59861 ext 274). There are guides to Genealogical Sources (1981) and the Archive Collections (1973) and leaflets on the "Probate Records of the Diocese of York" and on "How to Find a Will". Space is very limited and an appointment must be made in advance.

For the **Prerogative Court of York** there are printed indexes to wills and admons 1389-1688 (Yorks Arch Soc Record Series 4,6,11,14,19,22,24,26,28,32,35, 49,60,68,89). These indexes also include the Exchequer Court of York (see Yorkshire, right) and the **Court of the Dean and Chapter of York** (for which, 1321-1724, see also YAS 38). There is a TS index to P.C.Y. (only), 1688-1731; and MS calendars (jointly with the Exchequer Court), 1731-1857.

The Dean and Chapter had jurisdiction during archiepiscopal vacancies, but, except for the year 1724 (for which there is a contemporary calendar), records are calendared with P.C.Y.

For the **Chancery Court of the Archbishop of York** there is a printed index to wills, admons and invs 1427-1658 (the earliest in fact Exchequer Court wills) (Y.A.S.R.S. 73, erroneously entitled 'Consistory Wills'), but since then a number of additional Chancery wills and invs have been found. See also wills in the archbishops' registers, 1316-1822 (Y.A.S.R.S. 93); 1825-1857 (Borthwick Inst Bulletin, 1975, pp.39-42).

Apart from the areas listed below,

Cheshire was in the diocese of Chester;
Cumberland was in the diocese of Carlisle;
Durham was in the diocese of Durham;
Flintshire (southern detachment) was in the diocese of Chester;
Lancashire was in the diocese of Chester;
Northumberland was in the diocese of Durham;
Nottinghamshire was in the diocese of York;
Westmorland was in the diocese of Carlisle;
Yorkshire (all Ridings and the Ainsty of York [13]) was in the diocese of York.

In **Cumberland** the deanery of Copeland (3) was in the western division of the consistory court of the archdeaconry of Richmond (diocese of Chester), and the parish of Alston (2) was in the diocese of Durham.

In **Denbighshire** the parish of Holt (16) was in the diocese of Chester.

In **Flintshire** the peculiar of Hawarden (15) was in the diocese of Chester.

In **Lancashire** that part of the county north of the River Ribble (5 and 10) was in the western division of the consistory court of the archdeaconry of Richmond (diocese of Chester); and Aighton, Chaigley and Bailey (14) were in the diocese of York.

In **Northumberland** the peculiar of Hexham and Hexhamshire (1) was in the jurisdiction of the archbishop of York until 1837; and Tockerington (Thockrington)(1) was a prebend of York.

In **Westmorland** the deaneries of Kendal and Lonsdale (6) were in the western division of the consistory court of the archdeaconry of Richmond (diocese of Chester).

In **Yorkshire, North Riding,** the deaneries of Richmond and Catterick (8) were in the eastern division of the consistory court of the archdeaconry of Richmond (diocese of Chester); the parish of Sockburn (4), the peculiar of Crayke (12) until 1837, and the bishop of Durham's peculiar of Allertonshire (9) until 1846 fell within the jurisdiction of the consistory court of Durham; and the parishes of Brompton, Deighton, High Worsall, Kirby Sigston, Northallerton and West Rounton (9) formed the peculiar of Allerton and Allertonshire under the jurisdiction of the dean and chapter of Durham until 1846.

In **Yorkshire, West Riding,** the deanery of Lonsdale (7) was in the western division of the archdeaconry of Richmond (diocese of Chester); the deanery of Boroughbridge (11) was in the eastern division.

Although **Lincolnshire** was in the Province of Canterbury, some Lincs. wills and admons appear in the records of P.C.Y. or of the Exchequer Court (right). An index to these is at the Society of Genealogists (see page 25).

Yorkshire

Since 1858: Probate records for England and Wales are at the Principal Registry of the Family Division, Somerset House, Strand, London WC2R 1LP. Indexes to these (to 1928) are held locally at the West Yorkshire Record Office, Wakefield; Sheffield Central Lib. (prior notice required); and York District Probate Registry, Duncombe Place, York YO1 2EA.

The county was long divided into the civil divisions of the North, East and West Ridings; and the city of York and the Ainsty (the area immediately surrounding the city); but these disappeared in the reorganisation of 1974.

Registered copy wills proved at York (mainly North and East Ridings) 1858-1941 (indexed) will in due course be available at the North Yorkshire Record Office, York, and original wills proved at York since 1858 and at Wakefield (for the West Riding) 1858-1939 are at York District Probate Sub-Registry. Registered copy wills proved at Wakefield, 1858-1941, are at West Yorkshire County Record Office, Wakefield.

Before 1858: Yorkshire was in the province of York (for P.C.Y. see page 46) and mainly in the diocese of York. The only major exception was the western half of the North Riding and a few parishes in the West Riding, which were in the eastern division of the archdeaconry of Richmond, part of the diocese of Chester.

Northern testators are relatively rare in P.C.C. (see page 2), except for the Interregnum, for which there is a printed index, wills and admons, 1649-1660 (Y.A.S.R.S. 1).

Most probate records relating to the diocese, those of the **Exchequer Court** (the equivalent of a consistory court elsewhere), are now at

The Borthwick Institute, York (page 46).

The indexes to wills and admons are mainly in the same series as for P.C.Y. 1389-1688 (Y.A.S.R.S., see page 46); 1688-1731 (separate TS); 1731-1857 (MS calendar with P.C.Y.).

For the **Chancery Court of York,** which also had jurisdiction in Yorkshire, see page 46, opposite.

Parishes outside the direct jurisdiction of the exchequer court of York are listed on pages 48-51.

YORKSHIRE

The following parishes, chapelries and other places were at some or all of times outside the direct jurisdiction of the exchequer court of York. The civil division of the county into which each fell is shown by the initial letter in brackets following each name:

(A)=Ainsty of York; (E)=East Riding; (N)=North Riding; (W)=West Riding. Details of the exchequer court of York are given under 'Yorkshire' on page 155. Details of all other jurisdictions in the county are given under the Riding sections, and places may be located on the maps of each Riding. The peculiars of the dean and chapter, and of the dean, of York each covered a number of parishes; places in these and those subject to consistory or archdeaconry courts have the following keys:

AN=Archdeaconry of Nottingham (diocese of York); CC=Consistory of Chester; CD=Consistory of Durham; DC=Peculiar of the dean and chapter of York; DY=Peculiar of the dean of York; R=Archdeaconry of Richmond, eastern deaneries (diocese of Chester); RW=Archdeaconry of Richmond, western deaneries (diocese of Chester); SLH=Peculiar of St. Leonard's Hospital, York. The names of all other peculiars are shown in bold type and can be identified from the key letters.

The peculiars of St. Leonard's Hospital, York (SLH) and of Beverley (BG) had concurrent jurisdiction with the exchequer court over a number of parishes, ceasing by the mid-16th century. Likewise the jurisdiction of the dean and chapter of York (DC) over a few parishes faded out, although it continued in many others. In such cases where the exchequer court had later jurisdiction, these places are included in the following alphabetical list but are not shown on the maps.

Acklam, (E), LE 36
Acomb (A), **AC** 46
Airmyn (W), SN 96
Aldborough (N), DC 17
Aldborough (W), DC 70
Aldbrough (in Stanwick St. John) (N), **AD** 1
Allerston (N), DY 11
Allerthorpe (E), DY 52
Allerton and Allertonshire (N), **AE** 8
Allerton Mauleverer (W), R 77
Alne (N), **AH** 21
Altofts (W), **AL** 93
Ampleforth (N), **AM** 14
Anderby Steeple (N), R
Anston (W), LE 104
Appleton Wiske (N), R
Arkendale (W), K 76
Arkengarthdale (N), **AR** 4
Askham Bryan (A), **AS** 48
Askrigg (N), R
Asselby (E), HO 56
Austerfield (W), AN 101
Aysgarth (N), R
Balne (W), SN 96
Barlby (E), HO 56
Barlow (W), SE 90
Barmby Marsh (E), HO 56
Barmby Moor (E), DY & BA 52
Barnby (E), DY & **BA** 52
Barnoldswick (W), **BD** 81
Barton (N), R
Batley (W), **BE** 92
Bedale (N), R
Beeford (E), **BF** 43
Beilby (E), DY 52
Beningbrough (N), NO 23
Bentham (W), RW 68
Beverley (E), **BG**
Bielby (E), DY 52
Bilton in Ainsty (A), **BI** 44
Bilton in Holderness (E), BG
Bingley (W), CR 84
Bishop Wilton (E), **BS** 40
Blacktoft (E), HO 56
Blubberhouses (W), K 76
Blyth (W and Notts.), AN 101
Bolton (nr. Pocklington) (E), BS 40
Bolton upon Swale (N), R
Castle Bolton (N), R

YORKSHIRE

Boston (Spa) (W), **DC** 83
Bowes (N), R
Bramham (W), DC 83
Brandesburton (E), BG
Brantingham (E), HO 62
Brayton (W), SE 90
Brignall (N). R
Brompton (N), AE 8
Brotherton (W), DC 95
Bubwith (E), DC
Bugthorpe (E), **BU** 39
Burn (W), SE 90
Burneston (N), R & SLH
Burton Leonard (W), DC 76
Burton Pidsea (E), BG & DC 66
Carlton in Snaith (W), SN 96
Carlton Husthwaite (N), **HU** 16
Carnaby (E), SLH
Castley (W), K 76
Cattal (W), HS 78
Catterick (N), R
North Cave (E), SLH
South Cave (E), **CA** & SLH 61
Cawood (W), WI 87
Cayton (W), K 76
Chapel le Dale (W), RW 68
Cherry Burton (E), BG
Church Fenton (W), FE 86
Clapham (W), RW 68
Cleasby (N), R
Clint (W), K 76
Coneythorpe (W), K 76
Copgrove (W), R 73
Copmanthorpe (A), DC 49
Cottam (E), LA 34
Cottingley (W), **CR** 84
Coverham (N), R
Cowick (W), SN 96
East Cowton (N), R
South Cowton (N), R
Crayke (N), CD 19
Croft (N), R
Crossley (W), **CR** 84
Cundall (N), R 17
South Dalton (E), BG
Dalton on Tees (N), DC
Danby Wiske (N), R
Deighton (N), AE 8
Dent (W), RW 68
Dob Cross (W), CC 9
Downholme (N), R
Driffield (E), **DR** 38
Drypool (E), BG
Dukeswick (W), K 76
Dunnington (E), **DU** 51
Dunsforth (W), DC 70
Easby (N), R
Eastrington (E), HO 56
Ebberston (N), DY 11
Ellerburn (N), DY 11
Ellerker (E), HO 62
Elloughton (E), **WG** 63
Eryholme (N), R
Fangfoss (E), DY 41
Farnham (W), K 76
Fenton (W), **FE** 86
Fewston (W), K 76
Fimber (E), WG 37
Finghall (N), R
Finningley (W and Notts.) AN 101
Firbeck (W), LE 104
Forcett (N), R
Foston on the Wolds (E), BG
Fridaythorpe (E), **FR** & WG 37
Garsdale (W), RW 68
Gateforth (W), SE 90
Gate Helmsley (N), BG & O 27
Gildingwells (W), LE 104
Gilling (N), R
Gisburn (W), SLH
Givendale (E), DY & **GI** 42
Goathland (N), DY 10
Goldsborough (W), R 77
Goodmanham (E), DC
Goole (W), SN 96
Gowdall (W), SN 96
North Grimston (E), LA 33
Grindal (E), **GR** 32
Grinton (N), R
Hambleton (W), SE 90
Hampsthwaite (W), K 76
Handsworth (W), LE 103
Hardraw (N), R
Harrogate (W), K 76
Hartwith (W), MF 71
Hauxwell (N), R
Haverah Park (W), K 76
Hawes (N), R
Haxby (N), DR & ST 25
Hayton (E), DY 52
Heath (W), WB 94
Heck (W), SN 96
Over Helmsley (N), SLH
Helperby (N), DC 18

YORKSHIRE

West Rounton (N), AE 6
Routh (E), BG
Rufforth (A), SLH
Ruston (E), BG
Saddleworth (in Rochdale, Lancs.) (W), CC 98
Salton (N), **SA** 15
Saxton (W), SLH
Scorborough (E), BG
Scruton (N), R
Sedbergh (W), RW 68
Selby (W), **SE** 90
Sherburn in Elmet (W), FE 86
Shipton (E), WE 53
Shiptonthorpe (E), WE 53
Sigglesthorne (E), BG
Silsden (W), **SI** 82
Skelton nr. York (N), AH 24
Skipwith (E), HO 56
Great Smeaton (N), R
Snaith (W), **SN** 96
Sockburn (N), CD 2
Spennithorne (N), R
Stainburn (W), K 76
South Stainley (W), K 76
Stalling Busk (N), R
Startforth (N), R
Staveley (W), K & R 76
Stillington (N), **SO** 20
Stockton on the Forest (N), BU 26
Strensall (N), **ST** 25
Swindon (W), K 76
Swinefleet (W), SN 96
West Tanfield (N), R
Temple Newsam (W), **TN** 89
Thornton in Lonsdale (W), RW 68
Thornton on Spalding Moor (E), DY 52
Thornton Steward (N), R
Thornton Watlass (N), R
Thorpe Salvin (W), LE 104
Thorpe Willoughby (W), SE 90
Throapham St. John (W), LE 104
Tollerton (N), AH 21
Topcliffe (N), DC & SLH
Tunstall (E), **TU** 67
Ulleskelf (W), **U** & WG 85
Wadworth (W), **WA** 100
Wales (W), LE 104
Walkington (E), BG & HO 58
Walshford (W), HS 78
Warmfield (W), **WB** 94
Warthill (N), **WD** 28
Wath (N), R
Wawne (E), LE 59
Weaverthorpe (E), DC 31
Weeton (W), K 76
Weighton (E), **WE** 53
Well (N), R
Welton (E), HO 64
Welwick (E), BG
Wensley (N), R
Westerdale (N), **WF** 5
Wetwang (E), BG & **WG** 37
Wharram le Street (E), DC 33
Whitewell (in Whalley, Lancs.) (W), CC 79, 80
Whitgift (W), SN 96
Whixley (W), R 77
Wigginton (N), AH 24
Wilton (N), DY 11
see also Bishop Wilton
Wistow (W), **WI** 87
Withernwick (E), HA 60
East Witton (N), R
West Witton (N), R
High Worsall (N), AE 3
Wycliffe (N), R
Yapham (E), DY 52
York (A), DC 47
(Bedern,
St. Andrew,
St. John del Pike,
St. John Hungate,
St. John Ousebridge,
St. Lawrence, (also SLH),
St. Martin Coney Street,
St. Mary Bishophill Junior,
St. Mary Layerthorpe,
St. Maurice,
St. Michael le Belfry,
St. Nicholas,
St. Sampson,
St. Wilfrid)
also, SLH
(All SS. North Street, and
St. Giles Gillygate)

Yorkshire: East Riding and the City and Ainsty of York

(now mainly in Humberside; north and west border, incl. York, in North Yorkshire)

Since 1858: see Yorkshire, page 47.

Before 1858: The East Riding and the City and Ainsty of York were wholly in the diocese and province of York, and, apart from peculiars, in the jurisdiction of the **Exchequer Court.**

The records of this and of nearly all the peculiars are now at

The Borthwick Institute, York

See page 46 for indexes and records of P.C.Y., the **Exchequer Court**, the **Chancery Court**, and the **Court of the Dean and Chapter of York** (which had jurisdiction in 14 parishes in York, 2 in the Ainsty and 5 in the East Riding; see list pages 48-51).

The list on pages 48-51 shows which parishes lay in the many peculiars. The initials used as a key to these are shown in parentheses, right. The Borthwick Institute has recently compiled TS indexes to the wills, admons and invs in all of these peculiar courts, unless shown otherwise. The **Chancery Court** and the **Court of the Dean and Chapter** also had jurisdiction in many peculiars, and these are asterisked.

Published: "York Clergy Wills 1520-1600", ed. Clair Cross, York, 1984.

Peculiars:
Acomb (AC), 1456-1837.
Ampleforth* (AM), 1528-1827.
Askham Bryan (AS), 1715-1799.
Barnby (Barmby Moor)* (BA), 1610-1729 (thereafter, Pec. of the Dean of York).
Beeford (BF), 1561-1678 (Y.A.S.R.S. 68).
Bilton* (BI), 1591-1849.
Bishop Wilton, 1531-1842 (calendar only).
Bugthorpe* (BU), 1544-1831.
South Cave (CA), 1558-1579 (TS index), 1579-1843 (calendar).
Driffield* (DR), 1557-1852.
Dunnington* (DU), 1549-1729 (thereafter see the exchequer court).
Fridaythorpe* (FR), 1593-1730 (thereafter see prebend of Wetwang).
Givendale* (GI), 1661-1669.
Grindal* (GR), 1623-1629 (thereafter see exchequer court).
Holme Archiepiscopi* (HA), 1560-1836.
Howden and Howdenshire (HO), 1521-1857 (calendar only, 1598-1622).
Langtoft* (LA), 1520-1845.
Laughton-en-le-Morthen* (LE), 1548-1857.
Mappleton* (MA), 1571-1849.
North Newbald* (NN), 1496-1851.
Preston in Holderness* (PH), 1559-1837.
Riccall* (RI), 1549-1833.
Tunstall* (TU), 1557-1838.
(Market) Weighton* (WE), 1502-1857.
Wetwang* (WG), 1559-1850 (see also Fridaythorpe).

YORKSHIRE, EAST RIDING

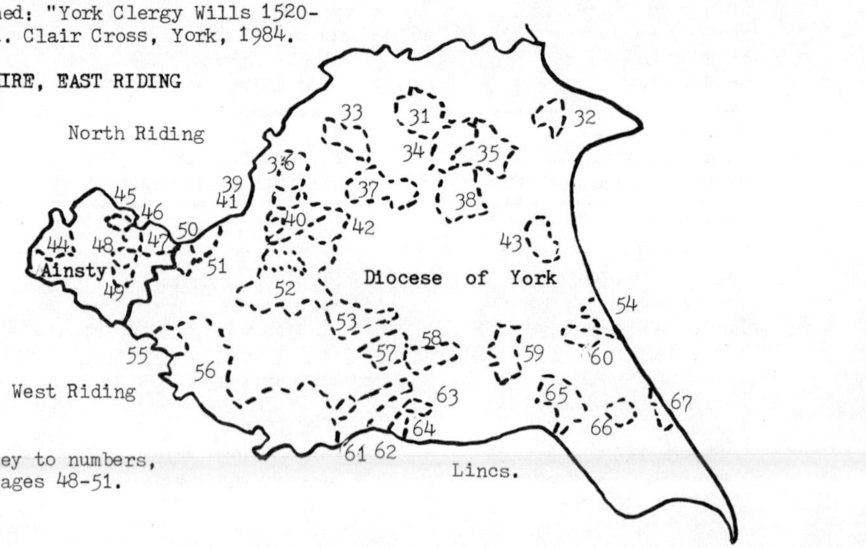

For key to numbers, see pages 48-51.

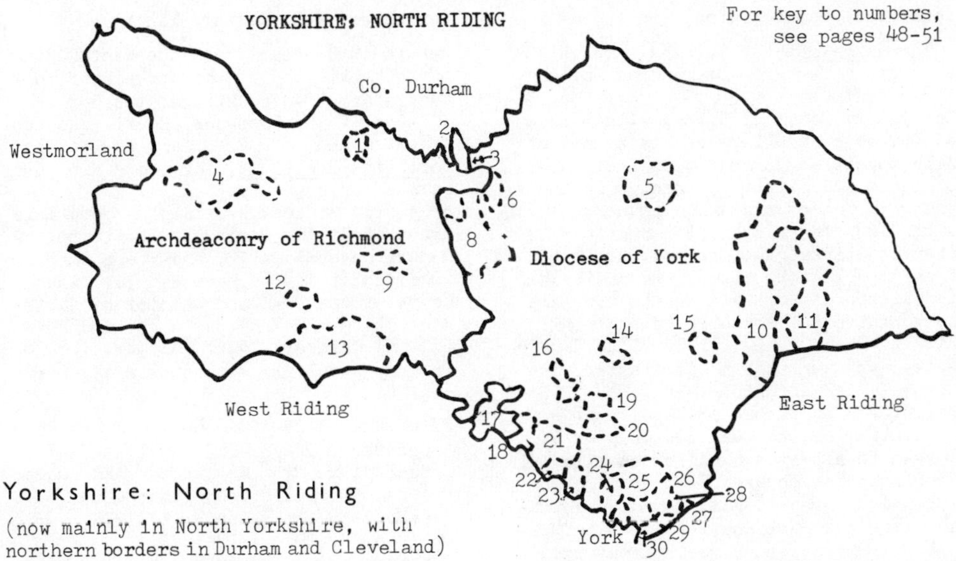

Yorkshire: North Riding

(now mainly in North Yorkshire, with northern borders in Durham and Cleveland)

Since 1858: see Yorkshire, page 47.

Before 1858: The North Riding of Yorkshire was split between the dioceses of York and Chester, both in the province of York. The eastern half lay in the diocese of York and was, apart from peculiars, in the jurisdiction of the **Exchequer Court**. The records of this, of P.C.Y. and of the **Chancery Court**, are at the Borthwick Institute, York, and are described on page 46. Records of the many peculiar courts, also at the Borthwick Institute, are detailed right.

The western half of the North Riding was in the **Archdeaconry of Richmond, Eastern Deaneries**, in the diocese of Chester. The records of this court are at Leeds District Archives (West Yorks. Archive Service), Chapeltown Road, Sheepscar, Leeds LS7 3AP (0532 628339).

The parishes in this jurisdiction (R) and in peculiars, are listed on pages 48-51. There is a 19th cent MS index to wills and admons, c1427-1857; and a card index, wills, admons and invs, 1521-1610, 1711-1750 (and in progress); also printed index, wills and admons, 1471-1616, A-G only (Northern Genealogist, vols. 3-5).

The Leeds Archives Dept. also holds indexed records of three N.R. peculiars:

Arkengarthdale (AR) 1698-1812; Masham (MF) 1571-1857; Middleham (MI) 1722-1854.

Records of most of the **peculiars** in the North Riding are at the Borthwick Institute, as described on page 52, and the places in them are listed on pages 48-51. The **Court of the Dean and Chapter** had jurisdiction in Helperby and Hornby in the N.R., and this and the **Chancery Court** had jurisdiction in many peculiars, as asterisked, see page 46.

Dean of York* (DY)(jurisdiction incl. 7 parishes in the North Riding), 1604-1722 (printed, Y.A.S.R.S. 73); 1531-1708, 1722-1857 (TS index).
Aldborough (in Stanwick St John)(AD), 1610-1700 (Y.A.S.R.S. 60)(in York Minster Library).
Alne and Tollerton (AH), 1458-1856.
Ampleforth* (AM), 1528-1827.
Bugthorpe*, 1544-1831.
Howden and Howdenshire (incl. Holtby in the North Riding)(HO), 1521-1857 (calendar 1598-1622 only).
Husthwaite* (HU), 1633-1661 (TS), 1661-1842 (calendar).
Linton on Ouse (LI), 1710-1735.
Newton on Ouse with Beningbrough (NO), 1614-1812.
Osbaldwick* (O), 1549-1827.
Salton* (SA), 1531-1826.
Stillington* (SO), 1515-1843.
Strensall* (ST), 1528-1640 (TS), 1640-1739 (calendar), 1740-1852 (TS).
Warthill* (WD), 1548-1837.
Westerdale (WF)(records now lost), 1550-1575, 1669-1765 (Y.A.S.R.S. 74).

Yorkshire: North Riding, continued

The University of Durham (see page 15) also has a few probate records for the North Riding:

Consistory Court of Durham with Bishop of Durham's Peculiars of Crayke and of Allertonshire: jurisdiction incl. Over Dinsdale and Girsby, townships in the parish of Sockburn (mostly in co. Durham); until 1837 the bishop of Durham's peculiar of Crayke (then in co. Durham but from 1844 in Yorkshire); and until 1846 the bishop of Durham's peculiar of Allertonshire in Yorkshire (containing Birkby, Cowesby, Hutton Bonville, Leake, Nether Silton, North Otterington, Osmotherly and Thornton-le-Street). In main index to Durham probate records.

Peculiar of the Dean and Chapter of Durham in Allerton and Allertonshire (AE) (jurisdiction covered Brompton, Deighton, High Worsall, Kirby Sigston, Northallerton and West Rounton, all in Yorkshire. These places were transferred to York diocese in 1846). Index, wills, admons and invs, 1666-1845.

Yorkshire: West Riding

(now split between West, South and North Yorkshire, with western border areas in Cumbria, Lancashire and Greater Manchester; and the eastern Goole area in Humberside)

Since 1858: see Yorkshire, page 47.

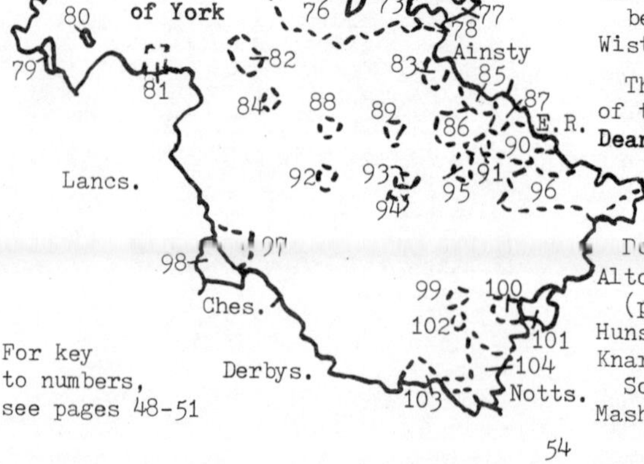

For key to numbers, see pages 48-51

Yorkshire: West Riding, continued

Before 1858: Nearly all the West Riding of Yorkshire lay in the diocese of York and, apart from peculiars, the jurisdiction of the **Exchequer Court.** Records of this, and of P.C.Y., are now at the Borthwick Institute, York, and are described on page 46.

Records of most West Riding **peculiars** are also at the Borthwick Institute, as described on page 52, and the places in them are listed on pages 48-51. The **Court of the Dean and Chapter** had jurisdiction in six W.R. parishes, and this and the **Chancery Court** had jurisdiction in many peculiars, as asterisked, see page 46.

Barnoldswick (BD), 1660-1794 (very few) (printed, Y.A.S.R.S. 118).
Crossley, Bingley, Cottingley and Pudsey (CR), 1586-1676 (some)(Northern Genealogist, 1); calendar to 1804.
Driffield* (DR), 1557-1852.
Fenton* (FE), 1528-1854.
Laughton en le Morthen* (LE), 1548-1857.
Marsden (MD), 1664-1855 (Northern Genealogist, 2)(also calendar from 1655).
Mexborough and Ravenfield* (ME), wills 1662-1740, 1760-1839 (calendar).
Selby (SE), 1555-1857 (calendar from 1681); 1634-1710 (printed abstracts, Y.A.S.R.S. 47).
Silsden (SI), 1588-1737 (Northern Genealogist, 1), 1737-1809 (calendar).
Snaith (SN), 1568-1857 (calendar).
Temple Newsam (TN), 1612-1701 (Northern Genealogist, 1; and Thoresby Soc. 33)
Ulleskelf* (U), 1612-1751 (see also prebend of Wetwang).
Wadworth* (WA), 1639-1819 (see also prebend of South Cave, East Riding).
Warmfield with Heath (WB)(location unknown), 1642-1691 (Northern Gen., 1).
Wetwang* (WG), 1588-1850 (see also prebend of Ulleskelf).
Wistow (WI), 1558-1842.

The Leeds Archives Dept. has records of the **Archdeaconry of Richmond, Eastern Deaneries**, which included all parishes in the deanery of Boroughbridge not in peculiars. Indexes, page 53, places listed on pages 48-51.

Peculiars at Leeds Archives Dept.:

Altofts in Normanton (AL), 1622-1677 (printed, Northern Genealogist 1).
Hunsingore (HN), 1607-1839 (MS).
Knaresborough (K), 1640-1857 (Surtees Soc. 110; also abstracts, 104).
Masham (MF), 1572-1857.

Yorkshire: West Riding, continued

The Lancashire Record Office, Preston has records of the **Western Deaneries** of the **Archdeaconry of Richmond.** These include four extreme north-west parishes in the deanery of Lonsdale (listed on pages 48-51). Wills and admons, 1457-1720 (19th cent calendar), 1720-1857 (calendar). Non-Lancashire parishes were omitted from L&CRS printed indexes.

Also at the Lancashire R.O. are records of the **Consistory Court of Chester,** whose jurisdiction covered the W.R. chapelries of Whitewell (in Whalley) and Saddleworth (in Rochdale), page 23.

The W.R. parishes of Rossington and parts of the Notts parishes of Blyth and Finningley in the W.R. were in the **Archdeaconry of Nottingham,** records partly at Notts. R.O., page 31.

The **West Riding Registry of Deeds** (founded 1704, now part of the West Yorkshire Record Office), Newstead Rd, Wakefield, has registered copies of some West Riding wills.

The Bradford Central Library has records of the **Manor of Batley**, 1651-1753 (Y.A.S.R.S. 74).

North Wales

ANGLESEY, CAERNARVONSHIRE, DENBIGHSHIRE, FLINTSHIRE, MERIONETHSHIRE, MONTGOMERYSHIRE

(now in Clwyd and Gwynedd; except Montgomeryshire, in Powys)

Since 1858: Probate records for England and Wales are at the Principal Registry of the Family Division, Somerset House, Strand, London WC2R 1LP. Indexes to these (to 1929) are held locally by the Gwynedd Archives Service, Caernarfon, and the Cheshire Record Office; for other copies, see page 1.

Registered copy wills from 1858 for all Welsh counties except Montgomeryshire are deposited at the National Library of Wales. Those proved at St Asaph (Denbighs, Flint, Merioneth) are indexed 1860-61, 1865-1923 and those at Bangor (Anglesey, Caernarvonshire) are indexed 1858-1930; 1931-41 in progress. Those for Montgomeryshire were proved at Shrewsbury and are deposited at the Shropshire Record Office.

Original wills proved at Bangor from 1858 and St Asaph, 1858-1928, are at the Bangor Probate Sub-Registry, Garth Road, Bangor, Gwynedd, tel. 0248 2410.

Before 1858: These six counties were in the province of Canterbury (P.C.C., page 2) and mainly in the dioceses of Bangor and/or St Asaph; but with a very few parishes also in the dioceses of Chester, Hereford and St David's.

Anglesey was wholly in Bangor.

Caernarvonshire was wholly in Bangor except for 3 parishes in St Asaph.

Denbighshire was mainly in St Asaph; with 16 central parishes in Bangor, and 1 parish in Chester.

Flintshire was mainly in St Asaph; with the 5 parishes in the southern detachment, and the peculiar of Hawarden, in Chester.

Merionethshire was in Bangor (22 parishes) and St Asaph (13 parishes).

Montgomeryshire was mainly in St Asaph, with 7 southern parishes in Bangor, 2 parishes in the archdeaconry of Brecon (diocese of St David's) and 9 parishes or parts of parishes in the episcopal consistory of Hereford.

Except for Hereford, the records of all these courts are at the

National Library of Wales, Aberystwyth (0970 3816-9)

Prior application should be made for a readers' ticket. A brief "Guide to Genealogical Sources" is available.

1. **Consistory Court of Bangor**, wills, admons and invs, 1635-1700 (index recently published by N.L.W.); 1700-1857 (MS calendar).
2. **Consistory Court of St Asaph**, reg. copy wills 1565-1623, 1637-1648; orig wills, admons, invs 1583-84,1606,1609, 1612,1623,1625,1627,1633-34,1636,1638-1647; wills, admons, invs 1660-1700 (card index in progress for publication; 1660-1729 (calendar, alphabetical by Christian name), 1729-1820 (card index, surnames), 1821-1857 (calendar, surnames).
3. **Consistory Court of Chester** (jurisdiction, Holt in Denbighs., and the southern detachment of Flint. Records relating to these Welsh parishes have been separated from those for the remaining, English, part of the diocese).

   Wills, admons and invs, 1546-1837 (Lancs & Ches R.S., see page 9).
4. **Archdeaconry of Brecon** (Kerry and Mochdre in Montgomeryshire - see p.57).
5. **Peculiar Court of Hawarden.** Wills, admons and invs, 1554-1800 (printed index, Flintshire Hist. Soc. vol.4, pt.2); 1801-1857 (unpublished index).

For a map of North Wales, see page 56.

NORTH WALES

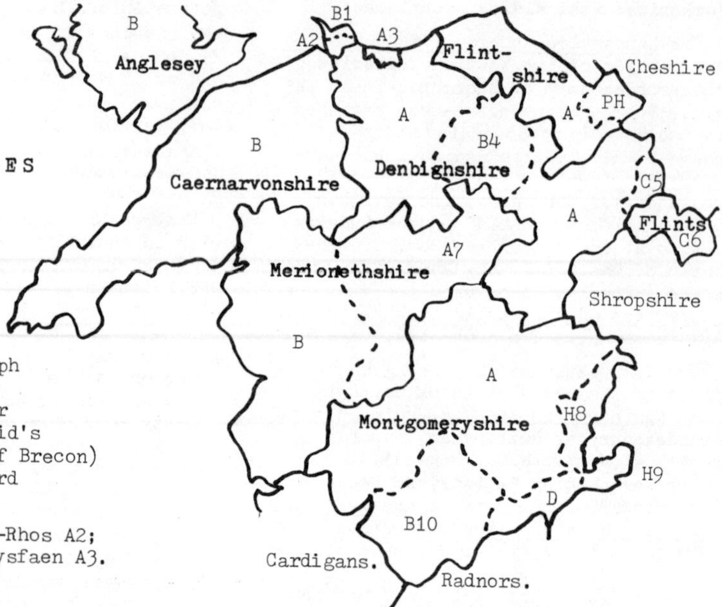

A : Diocese of St Asaph
B : Diocese of Bangor
C : Diocese of Chester
D : Diocese of St David's
(Archdeaconry of Brecon)
H : Diocese of Hereford

Caernarvonshire
Llandudno B1; Eglwys-Rhos A2; Llangystennin A2; Llysfaen A3.

Denbighshire (B4)
Clocaenog, Derwen, Efenechtid, Gyffylliog, Llanbedr Dyffryn Clwyd, Llandyrnog, Llanelidan, Llanfair Dyffryn Clwyd, Llanfywrog, Llangwyfan, Llangynhafal, Llanhychan, Llanrhaeadr-yng-Nghinmeirch, Llan-rhudd, Llanynys, Ruthin; Holt C5.

Flintshire
Peculiar of Hawarden (PH);
Southern Detachment (C6):
Bangor Iscoed, Hanmer, Overton, Threapwood, Worthenbury.

Merionethshire (A7)
Betws Gwerful Goch, Corwen, Gwyddelwern, Llandderfel, Llandrillo, Llanfor, Llangar, Llangywer, Llansanffraid Glyndyfrdwy, Llanymawddwy, Llanuwchllyn, Llanycil, Mallwyd.

Montgomeryshire
Alberbury (partly Salop) H8; Buttington H8; Carno B10; Churchstoke H9; Forden H8; Hyssington H9; Kerry (Ceri) D; Llandinam B10; Llangurig B10; Llanidloes B10; Llanwynog B10; Mainstone (partly Salop) H9; Mochdre D; Montgomery H8; Penstrowed B10; Snead H9; Trefeglwys B10; Worthen (partly Salop) H8.

North Wales, continued

For the **Episcopal Consistory Court of Hereford** (with jurisdiction over nine parishes in Montgomeryshire) see Hereford Record Office, page 19.

South Wales

BRECKNOCK, CARDIGAN, CARMARTHEN, GLAMORGAN, MONMOUTH, PEMBROKE, RADNOR

(now in Dyfed; Mid, South and West Glamorgan; Gwent; and Powys)

Since 1858: Probate records for England and Wales are at the Principal Registry of the Family Division, Somerset House, Strand, London WC2R 1LP. Indexes to these (to 1928) are held locally at the Glamorgan Record Office, Cardiff, and at Dyfed Archives Office, Carmarthen; for other copies, see page 1.

Registered copy wills from 1858 for all these counties are deposited at the National Library of Wales. Those proved at Llandaff (Monmouth and Glamorgan, except Gower) are indexed to 1905; at Carmarthen (Cardigan, Carmarthen, Pembroke and Gower) to 1941 and at Hereford (Radnor and Brecknock) to 1928.

South Wales, continued

Before 1858: These seven counties were in the province of Canterbury (for P.C.C. see page 2) and almost entirely in the dioceses of St David's and Llandaff, except for 8 parishes in the diocese of Hereford. Within the diocese of St David's the archdeaconry of Brecon had its own independent consistory court.

Carmarthen, Cardigan and **Pembroke** (archdeaconry of St David's) were wholly in the diocese of St David's and the jurisdiction of its consistory court.

Brecknock was wholly and **Radnor** mainly in the archdeaconry of Brecon and the jurisdiction of its consistory court; six Radnorshire parishes were in the diocese of Hereford and the jurisdiction of the episcopal consistory of Hereford.

Glamorgan was mainly and **Monmouth** almost entirely in the diocese of Llandaff; but 23 parishes in the Gower peninsula in Glamorgan were in the diocese and consistory of St David's (archdeaconry of Carmarthen); in Monmouth 3 parishes were in the archdeaconry of Brecon and 2 in the diocese and consistory of Hereford.

Except for Hereford, the records of all these courts are at the

National Library of Wales, Aberystwyth (0970 3816-9)

Prior application should be made for a readers' ticket. A brief "Guide to Genealogical Sources" is available.

1. **Episcopal Consistory Court of St David's: Archdeaconry of Cardigan** wills, admons and invs 1594-1747 (lists, chronological), admons 1700-1740 (index), wills and admons, 1746-1857 (calendar).
Archdeaconry of Carmarthen, wills, admons, invs 1594-1816 (chronological lists; 1780-1816 card index in preparation); 1817-36 (card index; separate card index to stray co. Cardigan entries); 1837-57 (calendar).
Archdeaconry of St David's, wills, admons and invs, 1594-1629, 1649-1653, 1700-1747 (chronological lists); admons 1700-1740 (index); wills, admons and invs 1746-1857 (calendar).
2. **Consistory Court of the Archdeaconry of Brecon**, wills 1570-1589, 1609-1658; wills, admons and invs 1660-77, wills 1694-1703 (calendars), wills, admons and invs 1733-1782 (endorsed 'not reliable'), 1783-1857 (calendar); 1678-1785 (chronological lists). TS index to pre-1660.
3. **Consistory Court of Llandaff**, wills, admons and invs 1575-1857 (calendar).

For the **Episcopal Consistory Court of Hereford** (with jurisdiction over two parishes in Monmouth and six in Radnor) see Hereford Record Office, page 19.

SOUTH WALES

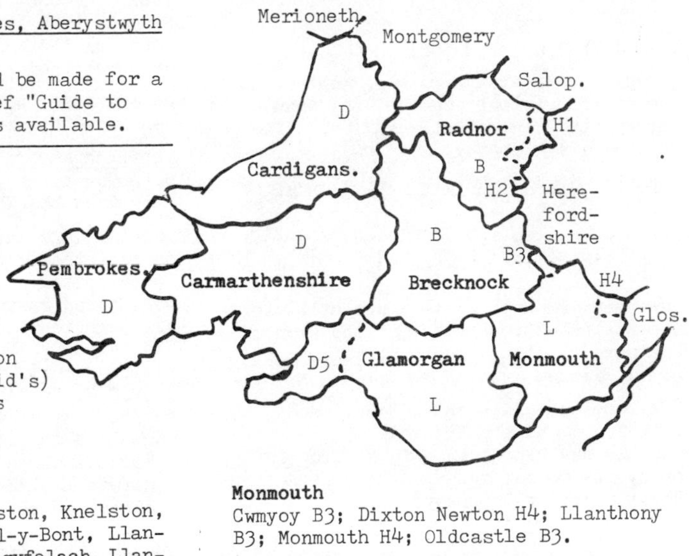

B : Archdeaconry of Brecon (Diocese of St David's)
D : Diocese of St David's
H : Diocese of Hereford
L : Diocese of Llandaff

Glamorgan (D5)
Bishopston, Cheriton, Ilston, Knelston, Llanddewi, Llandeilo Tal-y-Bont, Llangennith, Llan-giwg, Llangyfelach, Llanmadog, Llanrhidian, Llansamlet, Loughor, Nicholaston, Oxwich, Oystermouth, Penmaen, Pennard, Penrice, Port Einon, Reynoldston, Rhosili, Swansea.

Monmouth
Cwmyoy B3; Dixton Newton H4; Llanthony B3; Monmouth H4; Oldcastle B3.

Radnor
Discoed H1; Knighton H1; Michaelchurch-on-Arrow H2; Norton H1; Presteigne H1; Old and New Radnor H1.

Isle of Man

Since 1847: Probate records from the two courts which had joint jurisdiction in the island (see below) are in the Deeds and Probate Registry. From 1874 the Consistory Court had sole jurisdiction, and from 1885 testamentary business has been in the High Court of Justice. If the deceased lived or had property outside the island, then see also the Principal Registry, page 1.

Before 1847: The Isle of Man was in the province of York and the diocese of Sodor and Man.

Apart from P.C.Y. (page 46) and P.C.C. (page 2) all probate records for the island are at the

Manx Museum Library, Douglas (0624 5522)

These comprise the **Consistory Court of Sodor and Man**, from 1600 (index starts in 1659) and the **Archdeaconry Court of the Isle of Man**, from 1631 (indexed).

The two courts both had jurisdiction throughout the island, alternating for parts of the year, so it is necessary always to search both.

Channel Islands

Jersey: Probate matters were subject to the ecclesiastical court of the **Dean of Jersey** until as recently as 1949. The records are with the

Judicial Greffe, Royal Court, Jersey (0534 77111 ext 140)

and comprise: wills 1660-1964 (indexed) admons 1848-1964 (calendars).

Guernsey: Probate matters are still in the ecclesiastical court of the **Dean of Guernsey**, 12 New Street, St Peter Port (0481 21732).

The records, wills and admons, date from 1660, and are indexed.

Wills devising real estate, from 1841 only, are to be found in the **Royal Court of Guernsey**, The Greffe, Royal Court, Guernsey.

In cases where the deceased had property in England or Wales, see also P.C.C. (page 2). The Channel Islands were in the diocese of Winchester, but have always been administered separately.

Scotland

Since 1876: An annual consolidated calendar of confirmations has been prepared and, until recent years, printed. This can be examined in the Legal Search Room at the Register House, Edinburgh. Most non-current Sheriff court testamentary records are now deposited in the Scottish Record Office, unless still retained by the relevant sheriff clerk. Sheriffdoms, at first generally coinciding with counties, have now often been merged into larger groupings. The "Scottish Law Directory" lists the sheriff court districts and the parishes in each.

Since 1823: In this year the old probate jurisdictions of commissariots (see below) were abolished and replaced by sheriffdoms, at that time generally the same as the counties, though from the start Perthshire and Argyll were each split into two districts, and so was Angus from 1832. There are consolidated printed indexes to "Personal Estates of Defuncts" arranged in three groups: the Lothians, 1827-1865; Argyll, Bute, Dunbarton, Lanark and Renfrew, 1846-1865; and the remainder of Scotland, 1846-1867. The Scottish Record Office should be consulted on whether the probate records of the relevant sheriff court have been retained locally or deposited.

Before 1823: All pre-1823 records are deposited at the

Scottish Record Office, P.O. Box 26, H.M. General Register House, Edinburgh EH1 3YY (031-556 6585)

Until 1823 the various testamentary jurisdictions in Scotland were called 'commissariots', and the areas covered were based on the medieval dioceses, although the bishops' authority had been abolished in 1560. The principal commissary court, in many respects similar to P.C.C. in England, was that of Edinburgh, and, like that, should always be consulted in addition to local courts.

For the period 1801-1823 there are separate TS indexes at the S.R.O. for the commissariots of Edinburgh (to 1829), Glasgow, Peebles (to 1827) and St Andrews, and a consolidated TS index to the remaining commissariots throughout Scotland.

Indexes to all surviving testaments before 1801 have been published by the Scottish Record Society (SRS).

Scotland, continued

Commissariot of Edinburgh (jurisdiction over persons without fixed domicile or dying 'furth of Scotland'; locally in the Lothians until 1830.
Testaments, 1514-1800 (SRS 1-3, also BRS 16, 1514-1600).

Counties (numbers key to map), commissariot jurisdictions, starting dates of testaments, and SRS index volumes.

Aberdeen (10) and **Banff** (9): Mainly Aberdeen, 1715 (SRS 6).
Angus (or Forfarshire)(14) and **Kincardineshire:** Intermingled, St Andrews, 1549 (SRS 8); Brechin, 1576 (SRS 13).
Argyll: Mainland (16), Argyll, 1674 (SRS 9); The Islands (15) 1661 (SRS 11).
Ayr (34), **Dunbarton** (23) and **Renfrew** (28): Glasgow, 1547 (SRS 7).
Banff (9) - see with Aberdeen.
Berwick (32): Lauder, 1561 (SRS 18).
Bute (27): The Isles, 1661 (SRS 11).
Caithness (1) and **Sutherland** (2): Caithness, 1661-1664 (SRS 10).
Clackmannan (22) - see with Stirling.
Cromarty - see Ross.
Dumfries (39): Dumfries, 1624 (SRS 14).
Dunbarton (23) - see with Ayr.
East Lothian (Haddington)(31) - see with Edinburgh, above.
Edinburgh (Midlothian)(30) - see above.
Elgin (8) - see Moray.
Fife (2) and **Kinross** (20): Mainly St Andrews, 1549 (SRS 8).
Forfar (14) - see Angus
Haddington (East Lothian)(31) - see with Edinburgh, top.
Inverness (11): Mainland mainly Inverness, 1630 (SRS 4 and BRS 20). The Isles (6) - see Argyll.
Kincardine (12 and 13) - see with Angus.
Kinross (20) - see with Fife.
Kirkcudbright (40): Mainly Kirkcudbright 1663 (SRS 17).
Lanark: Glasgow, and Hamilton and Campsie, intermingled, north-west half of county (29). Glasgow, 1547 (SRS 7); Hamilton, 1564 (SRS 5 and BRS 20). The south-east part (35) in Lanark, 1595 (SRS 18).
Linlithgow (West Lothian)(26) - see with Edinburgh, top.
Midlothian (Edinburgh)(30) - see above.
Moray (Elgin)(8) and **Nairn** (7): Moray, 1684 (SRS 20).
Orkney and **Shetland**: Orkney, 1573-1615 (SRS 6), 1611-1684 (SRS 21)(Orkney); 1611-1649 (Shetland)(SRS 21).

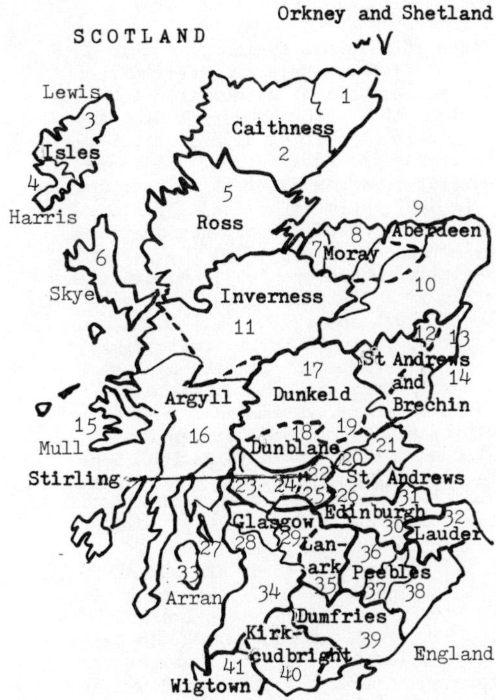

Peebles (36), **Roxburgh** (38) and **Selkirk** (37): Peebles, 1681 (SRS 12).
Perth: Northern part in Dunkeld (17), 1682 (SRS 16); southern part in Dunblane (18), 1539 (SRS 15); populous south-west parishes in St Andrews (19) 1549 (SRS 8).
Renfrew (28) - see with Ayr.
Ross and Cromarty (5): Ross, no early records.
Roxburgh (38) and Selkirk (37) - see with Peebles.
Shetland - see with Orkney.
Stirling and **Clackmannan:** Mainly in Stirling (25), 1607 (SRS 22); but see also Glasgow.
Sutherland (2) - see with Caithness.
West Lothian (Linlithgow)(26) - see with Edinburgh, top.
Wigtown (41): Wigtown, 1700 (SRS 23).

For the names of parishes in various jurisdictions (when a county is not entirely in one commissariot), see the relevant SRS volumes or "Wills and Where to Find Them".

Ireland

Since 1858: As in England, at this date probate matters were transferred from the ecclesiastical authorities to civil jurisdiction. The Principal Registry at Dublin also acted as a district registry for the Dublin area, and there were 11 separate district registries.

In 1922 the Four Courts in Dublin, the Irish Record Office, was destroyed by explosion and fire, and the Principal Registry records to 1903, and original wills from district registries, were lost. Fortunately the will books had remained in the district registries, though these do not contain copies of all wills proved. The consolidated indexes of wills and admons for both principal and district registries from 1858 also survived. The most serious loss is for the jurisdiction of the Principal Registry, the counties of Dublin, Kildare, Wicklow, Meath and part of King's County or Offaly.

The surviving records are now divided between the Irish Public Record Office in Dublin and the Northern Ireland Public Record Office in Belfast. The latter holds the records of the district registries of Armagh, Belfast and Londonderry, and these include the 19th cent records of cos. Louth, Monaghan and Donegal, all now in Eire. Records of the remaining district registries are all now at the P.R.O. in Dublin.

See also printed indexes for England and Wales, which include many Irish wills and admons - note that for 1858-1876 these are in a separate section following the letter 'Z'; and also see the Scottish Commissary Court.

Before 1858: Ireland was subject to the over-riding jurisdiction of the archbishop of Armagh, and within his province there were some 28 dioceses with the normal consistory courts and at least two peculiars. There were no archdeaconry courts. Virtually all the records of these courts were destroyed in 1922.

However, indexes or calendars to most survive in some form or other. In particular, the Irish Public Record Office has consolidated indexes of wills and admons from all Irish courts from October 1829 to 1879, and abstracts to 1839, originating in the Inland Revenue Office.

Indexes to lost records (if unpublished, at P.R.O. Dublin or Belfast):

Prerogative Court of the Archbishop of Armagh, wills 1536-1810 (printed); 1811-1857; invs 1668-1857; admons 1595-1802.

Counties and the main consistory court jurisdictions in which they lay:

Antrim: Mainly in Connor. Wills and admons, 1661-1857. Printed index to surviving records, 1818-1820, 1853-1857.

Armagh: Mainly in Armagh. Wills 1677-1857 (M-Y); 1687-1838 (C19 copy, Belfast P.R.O.); admons 1600-1857.

Carlow: In Leighlin. Wills 1652-1800 (Phillimore's Irish Wills 1); admons 1694-1845 (The Irish Ancestor, 1972).

Cavan: Mainly in Kilmore. Wills 1701-1857 (printed); admons 1701-1857.

Clare: Mainly in Killaloe and Kilfenora. Wills 1653-1800 (Irish Wills 3); admons 1704-1857.

Cork: Mainly in Cloyne. Wills 1621-1800 (Irish Wills 2), 1801-1857 (damaged), 1808-1838 (C19 copy), admons 1630-1857. And in Cork and Ross. Wills 1548-1800 (Irish Wills 2), 1801-1857, admons 1612-1857.

Donegal: Mainly in Raphoe. Wills 1684-1857 (Irish Wills 5); admons 1684-1857.

Down: Mainly in Down and Dromore, and the peculiar of Newry and Mourne. Wills, Dromore 1678-1857; Newry and Mourne 1727-1857 (Irish Wills 4); to surviving wills, Down 1850-1857 (printed). Down, wills, 1681-1856, admons 1684-1857; Dromore, wills 1801-1857 (damaged), admons 1749-1857; Newry and Mourne, admons 1811-1845 (Irish Ancestor, No.1, 1969, pp.41-42).

Dublin: In Dublin. Wills 1638-1857 (printed), admons 1697-1845.

Fermanagh: Mainly in Clogher. Wills and admons 1660-1857.

Galway: Mainly in Clonfert and Kilmacduagh. Wills 1665-1857, admons 1778-1857 (ptd, Irish Ancestor, 1970, 1974; also, 1664-1838, with additional information from Betham's copy, ed. P. Smythe-Wood, 1977). And Tuam, admons 1692-1857.

Kerry: In Ardfert and Aghadoe. Wills, 1690-1800 (Irish Wills 3), 1801-1857, admons 1738-1837.

Kildare: Partly in Dublin (for which see co. Dublin) and partly in Kildare. Wills 1661-1800 (Irish Wills 1; and in Jnl of co. Kildare Arch Soc, vol.4, no. 6), admons 1770-1848 (Jnl K A S 5, 3).

Ireland, continued

Kilkenny: mainly in Ossory. Wills, 1536-1800 (Irish Wills 1), admons 1845-1857 (printed).

King's County (Offaly): Mainly in Kildare (see co. Kildare) and Killaloe and Kilfenora (see co. Clare).

Leitrim: Mainly in Kilmore (see co. Cavan) and partly in Ardagh (see co. Longford).

Limerick: Mainly in Limerick. Wills 1615-1857 (Irish Wills 3), 1801-1857, admons 1737-1837. And Cashel and Emly, wills 1618-1800 (Irish Wills 3), 1801-1857, admons 1644-1857.

Londonderry: Mainly in Derry. Wills 1612-1857 (Irish Wills 5), admons 1698-1857.

Longford: Mainly in Ardagh. Wills 1695-1857 (Irish Ancestor, 1971); admons 1697-1850.

Louth: Mainly in Armagh (see co. Armagh).

Mayo: In Killala and Achonry. Wills 1698-1838 (from C19 copy), 1839-1857 (fragments only)(The Irish Genealogist vol 3, no 12); admons 1738-1837 (Irish Ancestor 7, 1, 1975, pp.55-61). And in Tuam, admons 1692-1857.

Meath: Mainly in Meath, Wills 1635-1838, admons 1663-1857.

Monaghan: In Clogher (see co. Fermanagh).

Queen's County (Leix): Mainly in Leighlin (see co. Carlow) and Ossory (see co. Kilkenny).

Roscommon: Mainly in Elphin. Wills 1669-1838, admons 1726-1857.

Sligo: Mainly in Killala and Achonry (see co. Mayo) and Elphin (see co. Roscommon).

Tipperary: Mainly in Cashel and Emly (see co. Limerick) and Killaloe and Kilfenora (see co. Clare).

Tyrone: Mainly in Derry (see co. Londonderry) and Armagh (see co. Armagh).

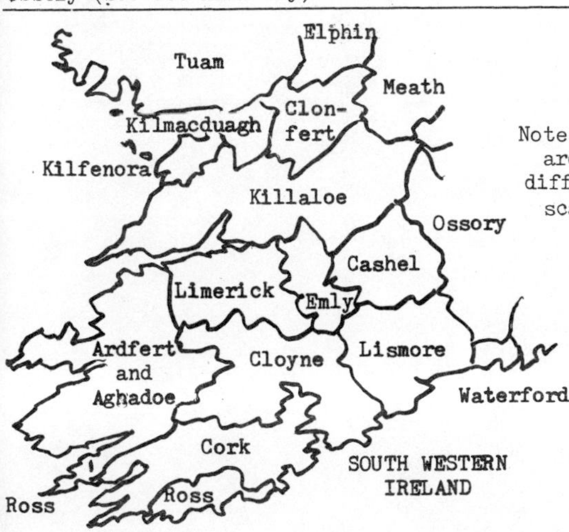

Note: Maps are to different scales

Ireland, continued

Waterford: In Waterford and Lismore, with peculiar of the dean of Lismore. Wills 1645-1800 (Irish Wills 3), 1801-1838, admons 1661-1857 (peculiar of Lismore 1766-1846 only).

Westmeath: Mainly in Meath. Wills 1635-1838, admons 1663-1857. Also Ardagh (see co. Longford).

Wexford: Mainly in Ferns. Wills 1601-1800 (Irish Wills 1), 1801-1857 (fragments), admons 1765-1833, grants of probate and admon 1847-1857. Also Dublin (see co. Dublin).

Wicklow: Mainly in Dublin (see co. Dublin). Also Ferns (see co. Wexford) and Leighlin (see co. Carlow).

Unlike English, Welsh and Scottish counties, those in Ireland rarely coincided exactly with probate jurisdictions. For more precise information, see "Wills and Where to Find Them". This also cites various sources for collections of surviving probate records.

Many testators also had property in England and Wales, and therefore may appear in P.C.C. (page 2) or P.C.Y. (page 46). Estate Duty Office will abstracts (mainly from P.C.C.) from 1821 to 1857 (and indexes from 1812) are at the Northern Ireland Record Office.